BUCKS COUNTY LIBRARY

HUD 1180/81

R
636.9323 M
KMW

ENCYCLOPEDIA OF GUINEA PIGS

MARGARET ELWARD

Distributed in the U.S. by T.F.H. Publications, Inc., 211 West Sylvania Avenue, PO Box 427, Neptune, NJ 07753; in England by T.F.H. (Gt. Britain) Ltd., 13 Nutley Lane, Reigate, Surrey; in Canada to the book store and library trade by Beaverbooks Ltd., 150 Lesmill Road, Don Mills, Ontario M38 2T5, Canada; in Canada to the pet trade by Rolf C. Hagen Ltd., 3225 Sartelon Street, Montreal 382, Quebec; in Southeast Asia by Y.W. Ong, 9 Lorong 36 Geylang, Singapore 14; in Australia and the South Pacific by Pet Imports Pty. Ltd., P.O. Box 149, Brookvale 2100, N.S.W. Australia; in South Africa by Valid Agencies, P.O. Box 51901, Randburg 2125 South Africa. Published by T.F.H. Publications, Inc., Ltd, the British Crown Colony of Hong Kong.

Introduction

The animal that is popularly known today by the names guinea pig and cavy is known to science as *Cavia porcella*. It is a rodent, belonging to the same order of animals as the squirrel, muskrat, hamster, mouse, rat, gerbil, beaver and many others. Within the order it is placed in the family of Caviidae, and the guinea pig is just one of a number of animals in the family, all of which are loosely known as cavies.

No one really knows why *Cavia porcella* is called the Guinea pig. It doesn't come from Guinea, which is in Africa, but from around Peru in South America, and it's not a pig. One theory about the origin of the name is that the "guinea" portion of it is a corruption of Guiana, the South American region that harbors *Cavia culteri*, the restless cavy, a rodent that looks somewhat like the guinea pig of today. Another theory is that British sailors returning from overseas used to sell our little cavy for a guinea, the gold coin worth twenty-one shillings; according to the proponents of this theory, the "pig" part of the name got stuck on because of a supposed similarity of the noise emitted by a frightened cavy to the noise emitted by a frightened pig. Perhaps the name, like so many others, is simply based on confusion. We do know that British sailors had introduced the rodents into England no later than the middle of the 18th Century, and we do know that these sailors often hit ports in both South America and the west coast of Africa on the same voyage before returning to England, so maybe the buyers of the cavies, knowing that the sailors had been to the Guinea region of Africa, just assumed that the cavies came from Guinea. Potential cavy buyers in England during the 1700's were not known for the exactitude of their taxonomy, and it wouldn't be taking too much for granted to credit them with calling the cavy a pig . . . to them it probably looked more like a pig than any of their other native animals.

The British, by the way, were not the first to bring cavies into Europe. The Spanish conquerors of Peru, the guinea pig's homeland, had brought them in by no later than the middle of the 16th Century. What they did with them we don't know; maybe they sold them for a golden Spanish coin, and for all I know the popular name for *Cavia porcella* in Spain today is *escudo puerco*.

Whatever the status of the guinea pigs in England and the Continent from about 1650 onward, there is good evidence to show that the little rodent was put to good use in its homeland. The Incas of Peru used to eat them, after first fattening them up by feeding them kitchen scraps. No Inca was allowed to be idle, and the old and infirm tribesmen (called *punucrucus,* or "old sleepers") were given the task of feeding and breeding the guinea pigs, which were kept in large numbers within the walled compounds of the Inca's houses.

Selection Of Your Guinea Pig

The guinea pig is cobby in type, which means that its rump or hindquarters is rounded. Its head is broad. The ears in pet stock guinea pigs are often high set, while those in pure show breeds are drooping; in both cases they are hairless. The eyes are bold and seldom blink. The legs are short; the front feet have four toes and the back feet have three toes. The length of the average guinea pig is 10 inches. Fully grown (about 14 months old) guinea pigs weigh between 2¾ and 3 lbs., but the weight can vary with the breeding status. A guinea pig has no visible tail, but the bone structure of a short internal tail can be felt at what is often called the 'tail stump.' Guinea pigs are bred in many colors, either 'selfs' (which means all one color) or mixed colors. The hair can be either smooth or rough and wiry and can be long or short.

When you select your pet guinea pig, do not pick the first pretty one that you see. You should always examine a pet for good health before you purchase it. There is nothing more upsetting for a child than to have his new pet die shortly after he has taken the pet home and has become attached to it.

It is best to purchase your guinea pig when it is six to eight weeks old, when it is fully independent of its mother. At this age, your pet will be readily adaptable to a new home and will be eager to make new friends. From this time to breeding season, your pet will be playful and kittenish in manners and you can enjoy watching it grow up.

A new cavy fancier may find a general cavy show a great help in the choice of the breed to keep. Himalayans are quartered in this section of a show in England. Photo by C. Eurich.

After you have picked the guinea pig that you think you want for a pet, examine it for health. It should weigh between eight and twelve ounces. Your cavy should be alert and lively. Its eyes should be large and brilliant, free from weeping and discharge. Its nose should be free of discharge too. Hold its nose close to your ear and listen for signs of wheezing and gurgling in its nose or throat. These are signs of a chest complaint, so if the cavy you are holding has these signs, select another one. Look at the feet and check the foot pads and claws. If they are caked in dry or wet diarrhea, it means that the cavy is suffering from a stomach upset that could result in illness. Look at its teeth and make sure that they are sound and unbroken.

A pair of cavies, a Dutch and a Self, in a show pen waiting for their turn to be judged. Photo by B. Seed.

Make sure your guinea pig has a good coat. Run your finger through its coat from rump to head and check for bare patches in the hair, dry or cracked skin and skin eruptions. Each type of guinea pig has an individual coat type. If you want an English, look for the sleek, satiny coat; an Abyssinian should have a rough textured coat with nine to ten noticeable rosettes; the Peruvian should have long, silky hair, clean and unmatted; and an American should have a short smooth coat.

Look at the litter of cavies before making your final selection. If young boars and young sows have been housed together after they had been weaned from their mother, it is possible that some of the sows will be pregnant. At this age, a pregnancy would be difficult for a sow since she has not matured enough to carry young or to give birth. There is a chance that if you do choose a sow from such a litter and she is pregnant, she could die.

An indoor hutch, compartments arranged in tiers, where several Dutch cavies are housed. Drinking bottles are fixed outside for easy access. Photo by B. Seed.

Housing Your Pet Guinea Pig

Like any other pet you may own, your guinea pig should have a home of its own. The type of guinea pig cage that is sold in most pet stores is usually not expensive. Most come equipped with a feeding dish, a watering dish, and a sliding bottom compartment that will make cleaning the cage easier for you.

Each guinea pig that you own should have a minimum of two square feet in its living quarters. It should not be cramped because its droppings should not be close to the feeding area. If you keep two guinea pigs in three square feet or three guinea pigs in four square feet, it would be the maximum crowding they could take without losing good sanitary conditions. Some breeders believe, however, that each cavy can get along well in a space of two feet by a foot square also.

The size of the cage will determine how often you will have to change the bedding. If you have only one pet in six square feet of bedding, you could go one month without having to change it. On the other hand, if you keep six pets in the same space, you will have to change the bedding every few days. Just keep in mind that the larger the area you supply for each pet, the less frequently the bedding will need changing.

Hay should not be used, unless it is fresh, clean and dry; beware of hay that is damp and moldy, or contaminated by other animal's droppings or chemicals. Photo by B. Seed.

For bedding, you should choose a material that is clean, dry and dust-free. You could use coarse sawdust, wood shavings, straw, rice hulls or hay. The hay is the best to use, but it should be fresh and dry, never damp and moldy. (It is also important to avoid hay which has been sprayed with insecticides, as these might prove toxic to the guinea pig.) Your guinea pig will tunnel through the thicker stems, nibble the tender stems and leaves, and eventually stamp down the parts too tough to eat. Its coat will become shiny from rubbing against the hay and, although it might possibly scratch its eyes a little on sharp stems, the advantages far outweigh the disadvantages. The eye scratches rarely need medication; in a few days they heal and don't seem to bother the animals. Oat straw is also good for bedding and for roughage. Many breeders in the United States prefer rice hulls as bedding.

Whether or not you plan to have your guinea pigs mate, you will need a nesting box. This does not need to be elaborate; wooden or card-board boxes are fine. If there is room in your pets' cage, provide a nesting box they can sleep in. Your pets will like their box dark, so leave the tops on and remove only enough of an end to let one force its way inside.

You can easily make a cavy cage yourself. Just make a wooden framework by attaching four uprights to a top frame and a bottom frame. Then cover the sides and one end with wire mesh. You can place a pan at the bottom.

Cavies kept in cages with exposed walls should not be kept outside all the time. These animals are easily chilled and can catch colds. Water is best supplied in a spouted drinking bottle to avoid possible contamination, and bedding must be provided also. Photo by L. van der Meid.

On warm sunny days you can take your pet outdoors. All you need to do is place the cage (without the pan) over your pets as above. They will safely munch on bits of grass, run, and enjoy the fresh air.

A cavy carrying or traveling box with hinged lid and wire mesh ventilators on three sides. Its small size makes it easy to move and clean. Photo by B. Seed.

In most parts of the country, it is not possible to house a guinea pig outdoors all year-round. Around Florida and the Gulf Coast, pet guinea pigs can be kept outside all year long, if the nest boxes are stuffed with hay for insulation. The boxes should be stuffed loosely with hay so that the guinea pig can create a snug nest, secure from the chilly night air. In other parts of the country, there are usually a few mild months during the year when guinea pigs would benefit from a temporary outdoor pen; however, they should be brought indoors before the frost. An outdoor rabbit hutch makes a perfect cage for your guinea pig.

Construction plan of a type of hutch suitable for keeping cavies indoors in a shed.

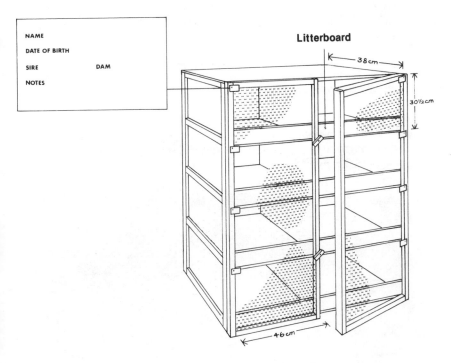

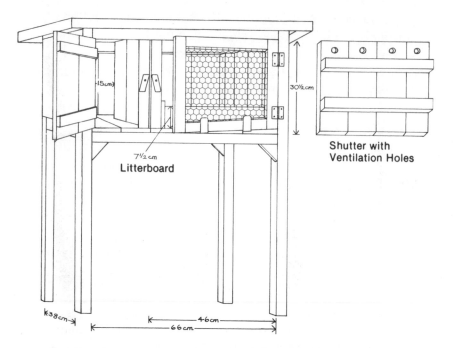

Shutter with
Ventilation Holes

Litterboard

Construction plan of a type of hutch suited for keeping guinea pigs outside the house. A movable shutter gives added protection at night and during bad weather.

By using removable separators, a large pen can house several cavies temporarily. However, the bottom must have bedding of some kind always. Photo by L. van der Meid.

Although an all-glass aquarium is clean and good-looking, it is not suitable for housing cavies. Due to poor air circulation, the animals can become overheated. Photo by M. F. Roberts.

If you are considering housing your guinea pig outdoors permanently or temporarily, there are a few things to consider. The cage should be protected from dogs, cats, rats and small children. Your guinea pig is not as agile as some household pets, so keep the top of its cage covered at all times to keep the other animals out. Even if the sides are high, it may decide to go visiting outside the cage and a fall could easily injure or kill it. Remember, too, that guinea pigs cannot adjust to wetness or to extended periods of cold. If you cannot provide it with a warm, dry nest box, don't keep it. Another important consideration is that guinea pigs are diurnal animals, which means that they like daylight. Your pet will love to bask in the sun, but you must provide some cool shade in the nest in case the sun should get very intense. Before placing your pet's cage, make note of the sun's path across your yard and place your pet's cage where it can enjoy the sun but not bake in it.

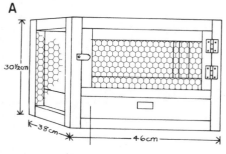

A

30½cm

38cm

46cm

Removable Tray

Construction plan of cages for cavies: A. "Bird cage" style suited for an apartment; B. Hutch wth removable section ("lawn run") for temporary use outside the main housing hutch; C. Hutch with bedroom and veranda (wired section).

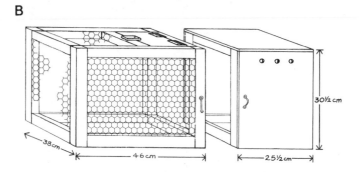

B

38cm

46cm

30½ cm

25½cm

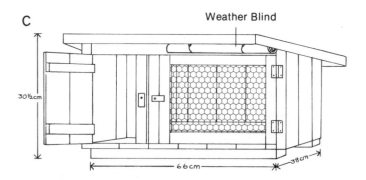

C

Weather Blind

30½cm

66cm

38cm

General Care

It is essential that your guinea pigs or cavies are fed at regular times each day, as they are animals that like a routine life. They are perfectly content when fed on a mixed balanced diet of herbage and dry mixed cereals. Hay and straw form a large part of their diet, and without these aids to digestion, intestinal upsets may arise. Water should always be available to them, although some do not attempt to drink because they find enough moisture in their food.

You need to keep their hutches draft-proof and to provide shelter for them in both winter and summer. Cavies can die from exposure to extremes in the temperature. A shed is preferred for them in the colder weather, but if this is not possible, a rain-proof hutch with a covered front is a necessity. They need to have sufficient bedding so that they can get under it for warmth.

If you keep your cavies in the house, the hutch must be placed away from radiators or hot pipes to prevent distress from the excessive heat. Whichever type of housing you choose, it has to be draftless, constantly dry and free from extremes of weather. Although in some parts of the United States cavies are kept outside, indoor cages are preferred and more common.

The hutches should be cleaned out weekly if they are kept out-of-doors and should be cleaned even more often if you keep them in the house. The sides and the bottom of the hutch need to be sprayed with disinfectant, but allow them to dry before you place your cavies back in the hutch.

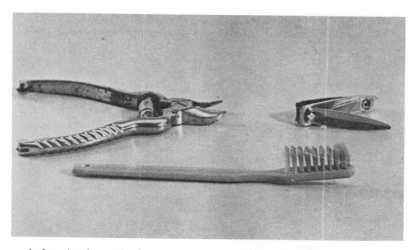

A few basic tools for keeping a cavy groomed: toenail clipper, fingernail clipper and toothbrush. Photo by M. F. Roberts.

When your cavy is over a year old, it will probably need its claws clipped and you must take great care when doing this. (Refer to the diagram of the sex organs which also includes the cutting of claws.) It is best to examine the claws thoroughly before attempting to cut them with the clippers. The claw must be cut above the blood vessels. Should you accidentally cut the vein, there will be excessive bleeding. Apply iodine to the toe if there is bleeding. (This can also be used for bleeding from torn ears caused by fighting.)

Your cavy needs brushing to keep its hair healthy. If you have any of the long-haired varieties, the brushing will keep their coats from becoming matted.

When your cavy's hair looks dull, dusty and greasy it has to be washed. You may also notice some small lice in the coat. These could have been in the coat when you purchased it or they may have come from poor quality hay. Washing will rid the coat of them. A reliable pet shop owner can recommend a dusting powder that will also kill the lice. You should apply it on the middle of the back, across the rump, behind the ears, under the eyes, around the cheeks, in the leg pits and on the back legs.

From time to time you will need to give attention to your cavy's teeth. If they grow exceedingly long they will cut into the gums and cause your cavy to have difficulty eating. You can cut the teeth with nail clippers, but you must be careful not to pinch or cut the lip or the tongue. Cutting will sometimes leave a jagged edge, so gently file the teeth with fine sandpaper after cutting.

Give your cavy twigs or hay cubes to gnaw and these will help to keep the teeth the correct length. Excessively long teeth can be caused when the general food they are given is too soft.

Any infection on the ear should be attended right away before permanent damage is produced and ruins the animal for showing. Photo by L. van der Meid.

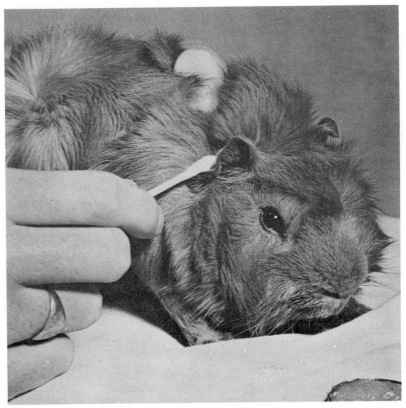

Always keep your cavy's carrying case free from dampness or the cavy might catch cold that can lead to pneumonia, which is generally fatal.

It is important that you realize that your cavy should not be transported in a trunk of a car as you travel to cavy shows. Many cavies die each year from inhaling the exhaust fumes of the engine while they ride in the trunk.

Your cavy will ask for very little in its animal ways, but it will give you a great deal of pleasure. A cavy will enjoy a long life span and good health if you take the proper care to see that it does.

Feeding

Feeding your guinea pig is a simple matter as guinea pigs are vegetarians and eat fruits and vegetables, guinea pig pellets, bread and will nibble on bits of dog biscuits. Guinea pigs will not eat what they do not like and among those things are onions, hot peppers and possibly some kinds of cabbage.

In one day, one adult guinea pig will eat the equivalent of one carrot, two stalks of celery, one leaf of lettuce, spinach or chicory, one small handful of hay, one lick of salt and one to twenty sips of water. A nursing mother might demand a little more and an old boar a little less.

Guinea pigs have a little peculiarity in their diets of which you must be aware. They must have a steady supply of vitamin C in their diets; a lack of this vitamin will result in scurvy, just as it does in man. You may buy complete diets in pellet form for your guinea pig, and these have a sufficient vitamin C content. There is a problem in buying feeds, however, because the vitamin C content decreases during storage. If the feed has been stored for more than ninety days, it may not provide enough vitamin C to maintain your pet's health. Unless you are absolutely certain that your feed is fresh and from a reliable source, you should supplement your pet's diet with fresh greens to ensure its health.

Some breeders and owners do not like to use green vegetables in the diets of their pets. Supplying green vegetables means extra work in feeding the pets and in cleaning the cages because the greens become spoiled and inedible. Many breeders stick to the pellets and water diet for the guinea pigs they breed, and they have no health problems.

As was mentioned previously, because of the uncertainty about the vitamin C content, we suggest that you give your pet sufficient greens in its diet. You must be careful, however, not to give your guinea pig too many greens. Constantly giving it too much will give it diarrhea. If it should get diarrhea, simply cut down the greens for a day. You may then give it half portions until the problem is eliminated. Too many greens will also make very loose waste.

Remember, too, that when using store-bought greens, you must wash them thoroughly to remove any harmful insecticides that may be present and could be harmful to your pet.

Dry foods for cavies are best kept in tightly closed containers to keep dampness and vermin out. All fresh foods should be scrupulously cleaned; dispense water in bottles with metal spouts. Photo by B. Seed.

For somebody who keeps only one or two guinea pigs, it is probably more convenient to purchase small amounts of packaged cavy food. Such foods are generally clean and fresh. However, supplements (vitamins) and green fresh foods must be provided.

If you keep just one pet, you must remember that it is a small pet with a small stomach, so do not give it an entire apple, a whole carrot, a half of a head of lettuce and a cupful of pellets for its daily meal. A good suggestion to follow is to take portions of the fruit or vegetable that you are using at your own meal and give them to your pet. You may give it a slice of apple, a piece of the lettuce leaf from your salad, a slice of carrot and a small piece of orange. You should remove anything that it does not eat every day and replace it with fresh food. You can vary the daily diet. Some of the vegetables that your guinea pig will like are carrots, carrot tops, raw string beans, potato slices or peelings, a portion of raw tomato and celery, just to name a few—it will even nibble on a dry or fresh ear of corn.

It is a good idea to provide your guinea pig with some dry foods in its diet. Most homes keep oatmeal on hand, so that is a convenient grain to feed to your pet. Occasionally, give

25

Shown is a manufactured cage for cavies. It includes a bedding of wood shavings, a drinking vessel (installed outside), a heavy feeding dish, and a bunch of hay for nibbling.

it just about one teaspoonful; this will be good for it. Other grains-barley, bran, whole wheat, corn meal and others-should be used proportionately.

If you are thinking of introducing new foods to your pet's diet do so sparingly. You can try foods like bread, crackers and shelled peanuts, but when you do, give it small amounts and eliminate one item from its regular diet. A cavy can only eat just so much and will waste anything that is left over.

For pets housed out of doors it is best in severe weather to give small quantities of roots and green food in the morning, then the food can be cleared up before it freezes in the hutch. Give extra mixed dry food, which should be fed at night, and allow the animal extra hay to burrow under for warmth. Little water is needed in the winter by the pet, as it will get moisture from the roots. When the weather is very cold, the drinking bottle on the hutch should be left only for short periods and not at night, as the water will freeze and expansion will cause the bottle to break.

Close-up of a drinking vessel with metal spout. Plastic and glass spouts are not recommended, because they can break and injure the mouthparts of your pet. Photo by M. F. Roberts.

You should use the heavy type of feeding bowl for your pet's food, the type that will not easily tip over. Keep a close watch on the bowl, because there are some guinea pigs that like to put their droppings in their feeding dishes. Make sure that your pet has a supply of fresh water at all times. Water bottles with the metal tips are the preferred type; guinea pigs like to chew a bit on the ends. Keep a close watch on the water bottle too. Your pet may blow water back up into the bottle and foul the rest of his supply.

Generally, it is not difficult to keep your pet well fed. If you notice that there is a lot of food left over, then you are feeding it too much. If all of its food is gone, even all of the vegetable, and your pet seems to be searching for something to eat, then you are not feeding it enough. Within a few weeks time you will be able to judge just how much food to leave for your pet without waste and spoilage.

Breeding

You can enjoy great pleasure from breeding your cavies as pets or breeding pure breeds for exhibition. Before trying to have your pet breed, there are certain details that you must be familiar with.

After you have watched your cavy mature, you may decide to mate it. When you originally purchased your pet, you may have selected it on the basis of health and appearance, not on its sex. You will now need to closely examine your pet in order to determine which sex it is.

SEXING YOUR CAVY

When examining a boar or a sow for sexing, it is best to hold the cavy with the right hand across the chest with your thumb and forefinger around the neck. Keep the shoulders against your chest and rest the rump in your cupped left hand so that the stomach faces upwards. Now the sex organs can easily be examined. (See diagrams)

If your pet is a boar, you will notice that there is the back passage or anus (A). In front of the anus there is a rounded area (B) in which the penis is inwardly encased, bordered by the internal scrotum. If you press gently at (C) on his abdomen, the penis will protrude. When examining a sow it will be seen that in front of the anus (D) there is hairless skin, shaped like an upside down "Y" covering the vagina (E, F and G); in front of the vagina there is a very small opening or slit which is the urethera or bladder exit (H).

WHEN TO BREED

You could breed your pet guinea pig when it is one or two months old, but that would be a mistake. Your sow should be six months old before mating and should weigh about one and one-half to two pounds. If she were any younger, a pregnancy would be harmful to her health and would leave the resulting litter in frail shape. Your boar should be at least eight months old before he is bred, again for health reasons.

The breeding pair should be in good condition but not over-weight. They should be well grown for their ages. Small, stunted parents usually produce poor quality offspring.

You may have read that it is not known how cavies mate or that they only do so at night, in the privacy of their cages. This is a fallacy. A cavy cannot mate unless it is in season.

What actually happens in the breeding cycle of a sow cavy is that she will come into season about every eighteen days and will accept mating for a few hours. As your sow comes into season, the part of her sex organs (see diagram) marked (F) and (G) become slightly swollen or enlarged and limp. The skin of hymen between these unseals to allow for penetration by the boar. If your sow is making her "purring" or mating call, she will often mate immediately or within a few hours. Once a series of mating acts has taken place, it is all finalized by the boar producing a waxy core or stopper that blocks the vagina. Your boar and sow will no longer have the desire to mate once this has been done, not until, of course, the young have been born and the sow is once again in season. After the mating has been completed, the hymen reseals until the young cavies are born, about sixty-five to seventy days after the mating has taken place.

It is best when breeding your cavies to arrange that the young ones arrive between March and September. During early spring there is an abundance of wild herbage which is very beneficial to your sow for lactation. The best times to begin mating your sows and boars are from January onwards. Litters bred in late autumn and winter are very slow

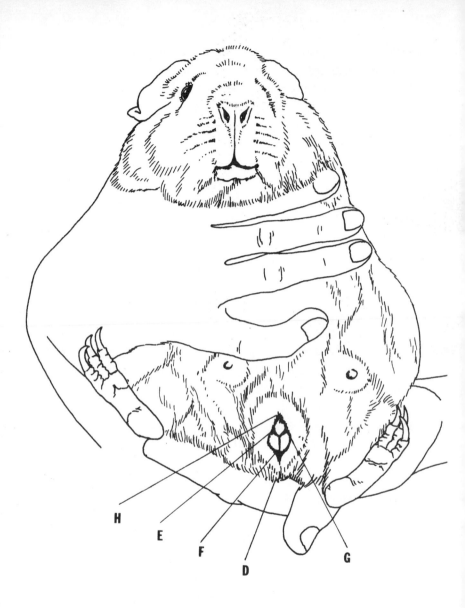

Diagrammatic illustration of the genital area of a female cavy: D. Anus; E, F and G. Hairless areas; H. Urethral opening.

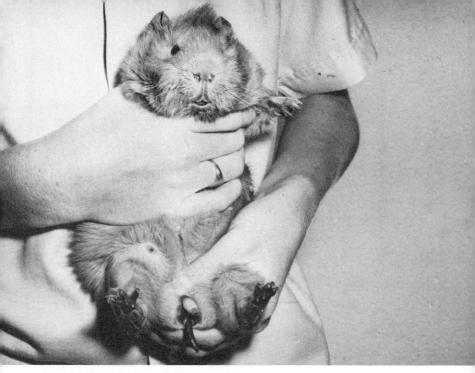

A male cavy. During the process of sexing a cavy it is possible for some excrement to come out also. Photo by L. van der Meid.

in growing and seldom have the stamina of the ones bred in spring and summer. However, the quality of the litter will not be affected much if they are kept in hutches indoors with the temperature regulated throughout the year. So, the time of the year for breeding is not of great importance.

BREEDING PROCEDURES

The breeding procedure used for cavies kept for showing is different from that used for cavies kept simply as pets. This comes under different categories including inbreeding, line-breeding and outcrossing. Inbreeding means that the mating cavies are closely related. Initially, a boar and a sow that have the outstanding qualities of the breed are purchased. These two are mated. From this mating, the daughters are mated back with the father and the sons are mated back with the mother. On rare occasions the sister

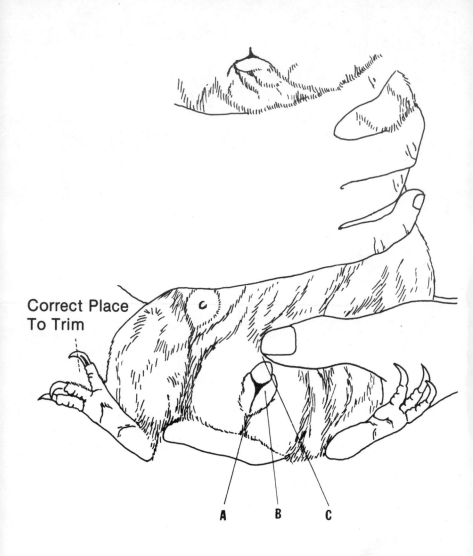

Correct Place To Trim

A   B   C

Diagrammatic illustration of the genital area of a male guinea pig and the correct place to trim the claws without cutting a blood vessel. A. Anus; B. Scrotal sac area; C. Point of pressure to cause protrusion of penis.

A cavy when properly held will not struggle; if comfortable, it will snuggle and settle quickly. Cavies are generally docile and will seldom bite. Photo by Brian Seed.

Smell plays an important role in the mating process of cavies. The White Abyssinian at the left is the female. Photo by G. S. Axelrod.

cavies are mated with their brothers. If the desired quality has a fault in the lineage, this very close mating is used to try to rectify it.

Line-breeding is again the mating of close relationships, but it is based on a plan different from inbreeding. All in the stud (the term used to describe the group of cavies that are kept) must be related and resemble a cavy to standard rules. Any cavy that carries bad faults must be eliminated. The cavies with better quality will be kept for future breeding stock and bred for the good points.

Another method of breeding is outcrossing. With this method, a boar or a sow having no relation to those cavies in the stud is brought in to try to rectify a fault that cannot be bred out by using the inbreeding method. It is well known that outcrossing or chance breeding will often produce a good exhibit in a first litter of pure breds.

The male is about to mount the female from the rear. Photo by G. S. Axelrod.

A successful mating is possible only if the female is in the receptive stage; if she is not the male will be driven away. Photo by G. S. Axelrod.

Cavies are gregarious animals, and many of them like to be petted. However, those that are sick or injured will not welcome handling.

Opposite upper photo: Two young British girls photographed at a cavy show. Note the certificates of award; one of them shows that the cavy placed second in its class. Photo by Brian Seed. **Opposite lower photo:** Fresh air and exercise are good. Allowing your pets to roam on grass gives them the opportunity to nibble fresh grass and to stretch their legs.

SIRE :_____	NAME_____	STRAIN :_____
DAM :_____	SEX :_____ BORN _____	BREED :_____
GRD. SIRE _____ Male	5 mths old on :_____	MARKING ETC.____
GRD. DAM_____ Side		_____
GRD. SIRE _____ Sow's		
GRD. DAM_____ Side		

SHOWING DETAILS	BREEDING DETAILS

Accurate breeding records are indispensable. Important information is indicated in this sample of a breeding form.

Any method of breeding must be based on a plan. There are many books available on breeding methods that are worth reading.

KEEPING BREEDING RECORDS

If you are going to breed your cavies, it is essential that you keep a history of the breeding stock. A cavy cannot wear a ring on its leg for identification in the way a rabbit can. A cavy's hock or heel is slender and the ring would slip off. You will have to make a hutch card for each of your cavies. On this card you should print the cavy's name or number, the breed, the date of birth, the parentage (sire and dam), and provide some space in case you would like to add some notes.

Your cavies' names together with the other details should be entered in a stud book for reference. You should always keep your stud book up to date, as reference to it will be needed often in the planning of your stud.

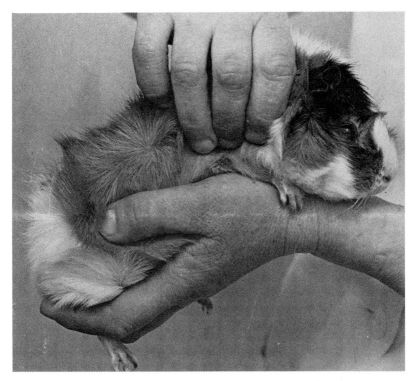
The proper way of holding a cavy.

BREEDING

There is no need to examine the sow to see if she is in season before breeding. Your sow and your boar should be kept together for 36 days. During this time your sow will come into season twice. If your sow and boar did not mate during your sow's first cycle, then they will probably do so during her second cycle.

The practical thing for you to do is to let your two cavies live together until you notice that your sow is pregnant. To be certain that she is pregnant, you can make a slight examination. Hold your sow around her shoulder with one hand and slide your other hand under her to the lower flexible part of her body where some fullness should be felt. If your

Four varities of Selfs are seen in these photos: Black, Chocolate (at upper center), Cream and Lilac. The Lilac has pink eyes; all the others have dark eyes. Photos by Brian Seed.

A group of cavies with different colors and textures of coat, and eye color.

A black-eyed Self White boar. With age the fur can darken so that an adult specimen may appear yellowish or dingy. Photo by David Whiteway.

sow is over five weeks pregnant, there should be movements of the unborn young ones. If she is over six weeks pregnant, the outline of the bone structure of the babies is very pronounced.

Once you are certain that your sow is pregnant, it is best to remove her from the boar and let her live on her own. If she remains with the boar, she will mate again shortly after her litter is born. This often results in the babies being trampled, and some could die. Another consideration is that if your sow has to rear her young ones while being pregnant her health will suffer.

It has been said that a good sow can have five litters in a year but it would be very cruel to allow your sow to have so many litters—she would be pregnant during all but two weeks of the year. Sows are not breeding machines and no sow should be bred in this way. Whether pure breed or pet, your sow's litters should be spaced so that she can have a rest and gain condition before being placed into the breeding pen again.

You should give your sow at least one month's rest before considering mating her again. Those that have large litters need even more time. Two to three litters a year is all that should be demanded from a sow, either as a pet or exhibition breeder. You will see that after your sow has had her first litter and has rested for a month or so, she will have grown considerably.

Planned litters from a pet cavy will give you a lot of pleasure as you watch their various stages of growth. You should find good homes for the surplus ones as soon as they are weaned from their mother so that you do not become over-stocked. The pleasure of having pet cavies will be diminished somewhat if you allow their breeding to get out of hand.

Small advertisements in local newspapers or on local bulletin boards reading "Free baby guinea pigs" makes sad reading, for many of these free would-be pets are destined for a short life. Some people take them on the spur of the moment with little knowledge of how they should be looked after. The new owner may tire of them easily and they change hands rather quickly; some even die from being treated improperly.

If you are breeding for a hobby, you will need a number of sows. The sows that you purchase should be the best quality of their variety. The breeding procedure will be the same as was previously given, but for the purpose of breeding the sows will be divided up into what are known as breeding pens. These divisions can consist of just a boar and a sow, called a pair; two sows and a boar, called a trio; and three or more sows and a boar, called a pen. As many as six or more sows can be housed together with one boar. It should be noted, however, that only one boar can be housed at a time with your sows. If you keep more than one in the pen, there would be vicious fighting, and this might result in injury or death to all the cavies in the pen.

When a breeding pen is made up of six sows and a boar, each cavy should have its hutch card attached to the hutch. There is always some characteristic about each cavy that will help you to distinguish each one.

THE PREGNANT SOW

When a sow becomes pregnant, you should remove her from the pen and put her in a separate hutch, along with her hutch card. If you do not want to go to this trouble, you may allow several sows to stay together to have their young but this could cause trouble or setbacks. Due to the eighteen-day breeding cycle, all of the sows would not have their young ones on the same day. It has been found that when one sow's young are born, it can cause another pregnant sow living with her to have a premature birth, resulting in weak and dead babies. However, some sows in a likewise situation will carry their young until it is the right

A Self White cavy. This show cavy has good ears; they are well-shaped and not crinkled at the edges. Photo by Brian Seed.

The competition for best Self Black show cavies is intense. A cavy with an extra feature such as large size, can have an edge over other qualified entries.

A Self Black sow. A boar or a sow when exhibited is judged on the same merits. Photo by Brian Seed.

time for giving birth. One sow may allow another's young to suckle her and yet another will not even allow another's young to come near her. The safest and surest way to breed is to transfer each pregnant sow into her own hutch. In this way her young will not become confused with the young of another, and you will also be able to keep a more accurate stud history.

Some people replace the pregnant sows in the breeding pen with sows that are ready for breeding. These new members must be watched because severe fighting can sometimes occur between them and pregnant sows that might still be in the pen. Such disturbances can cause abortions or miscarriages. It is best to set up fresh breeding pens where the cavies can all settle down within a day or so. Sows are inclined to fight, but the boar will come between them and try to stop them. A sow is known to fight a boar in the breeding pen as well. Always be careful if you try to stop cavies from fighting, for you can be badly bitten. If one of your sows is continually attacked by another sow, take her out and house her with a different boar. Continual biting can produce an abscess.

ABORTIONS

Some sows will stay in your breeding pen for many months and still not become pregnant. Watch these closely for light traces of blood on their noses. This could be evidence that a pregnancy was aborted and the sow had cleaned herself. Such a sow will not be feeling very ill, so it cannot be detected by loss of appetite. Loss of appetite is one of the first signs of illness in a cavy.

This type of sow loses her young ones about the thirty-sixth day of pregnancy. She will re-mate on the same day and will again lose the babies in the next pregnancy. If you see that your pregnant sow has blood on her nose or a bloody discharge from the vagina, house her on her own. With a little extra rest she will have a chance to carry her young to full term. If she again loses them, do not keep her as a breeding sow. Through weakness of the womb, some sows cannot carry their young to full term.

INFERTILITY

Some sows do not become pregnant because they are unproductive, or barren. There are those who never come to season and others who produce only one baby a year. These types are setbacks when breeding is taken seriously.

The boar can also be a cause of your sows not being pregnant. In this case you will find your whole breeding pen to be affected and you can lose many months in the breeding program. Your sows will be giving their mating calls and your boar will carry out a series of matings, but your sows do not become pregnant. What happens is that the boar does not fertilize the ova, or eggs of your sow. You must examine your boar, expecially if he is extra large in size. Often the very large boars are sterile. Do the same test you did for determining the sex for your pets; that is, push in on his abdomen to make his penis extend. Once the penis has been extended, look at the end for two horns or prongs. If these horns are uneven in length or if one is missing, your boar will mate but not fertilize. Some boars do not have this fault and yet are naturally sterile.

Other setbacks that can arise during breeding are:

1. The whole litter might be neglected at birth and all of the young die.
2. The sows could have difficult births when the babies arrive with the back feet first instead of the nose first.
3. The nose and face can get tucked under before birth. This causes the top of the head to come first and the baby will die as will those that follow.
4. Very heavy pregnant sows may die just a few days before the litter is expected.
5. Some sows may die from cold or damp drafty cages.

The eye color of the British Self Lilac is pink and in the United States ruby or pink. Photo by Ray Hanson.

A Self Lilac boar. Lilacs tend to have coarse coats which can be made to appear smoother by careful grooming. Photo by Brian Seed.

Cavies like to snuggle into their bedding or anything else for warmth.

A Self Lilac sow and her young. Lilacs are born dark but become lighter with growth. Photo by Brian Seed.

6. Sometimes the breeding plan will become disrupted when a stud boar is lost and cannot be replaced by one of the same lineage.

Anyone who keeps cavies as a hobby should know that many obstacles must be faced. You may, at times, feel like giving up your guinea pig hobby, especially after suffering several setbacks in succession. You must have determination to carry on and have patience in breeding your stud.

Once a cavy has become pregnant, the term "in-pig" is used and we will be using that term from here on.

GESTATION

After conception has taken place, gestation can take anywhere from sixty-five to seventy days. If your in-pig sow is going to have an average-sized litter, she will show her condition at about four weeks. She will be rapidly increasing in size and should be handled as little as possible. Cavies, having very flexible bodies, can be easily hurt internally and rough handling would induce an abortion or a miscarriage. Your sow would then become very ill and could possibly die after a miscarriage.

From the time that your sow begins to show, she will rest a great deal of the time. She should have plenty of water, vegetables and dry food. The dry food may have to be cut to half the amount, otherwise she will become too fat and may have difficulty giving birth.

You need not supply a nest for your sow to have her babies in, as they are not born naked like many other animals. When the young ones are born they are miniatures of their parents: fully haired, with whiskers, claws, teeth and open eyes. The average litter is three or four, and quite often, six. There are exceptions of more, but in those cases usually there are a few dead ones.

If the babies are born before the sixtieth day of gestation, they are premature. They will be very small and rather weak. Their hair will be very short and just protruding through the skin, a clear indication that they are premature. The mother will be very weak and will not eat, so be prepared to tempt her to eat with tidbits. All she will do is sit in the corner of her hutch with her tiny babies under her until she has gained the strength she lost through loss of blood. A premature birth is a semi-illness for a sow.

BIRTH AND THE NEWBORN

During the period of gestation the babies are enveloped in a membrane and are protected by a fluid. When the sow is ready to have her young and her labor pains begin, she will continually strain with each contraction. As she strains, she will push the baby's head forward through the vagina. As the baby's nose appears, the sow bends under and breaks the membrane by biting it. The fluid is released and the baby begins to breathe on its own.

If the sow does not break the membrane, or if it is not broken once the baby has left the mother's body, the baby will die of suffocation. Death in this way is the cause of the large loss of new-born cavies and it is such a disappointment for those who keep cavies as a hobby. Many people think that their sow gave birth to a stillborn baby when in actuality the sow did not break the membrane and the baby could not breathe. The sow will sometimes clean away the membrane after it is too late and often will not clean it away at all.

If you should happen to be present while your sow is giving birth, you may be able to save a baby that would otherwise suffocate. If you see that a baby is still enveloped in the membrane, you can revive it by breaking the membrane over the nose, opening the mouth and blowing in quick succession down the throat. At the same time, move the legs to cause exertion to get the heart and the lungs moving; if the baby gasps, there will be hope for it. Now warmth will be essential, so keep it in your cupped hands and continue to blow down its throat. Gently rub the hair with cloth to dry

A young Self Beige cavy.

Self Beige cavies are bred in many shades, but the shade preferred by exhibitors is a light medium beige.

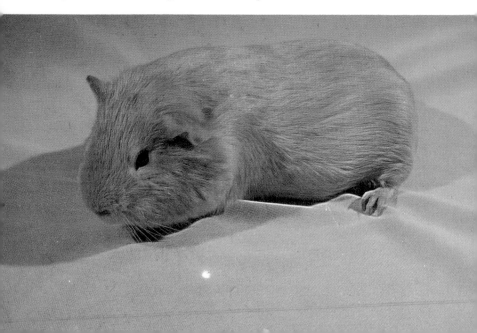

This Silver cavy has light circles around the eyes. Such circles are faults in ticked cavy varieties; the ticking should reach the rim of the eyes.

A young Self Golden cavy. Like the Lilacs, Self Goldens are born very dark, so they are not shown at a young age. The lighter coat of adults should resemble a golden guinea coin. Photo by Ray Hanson.

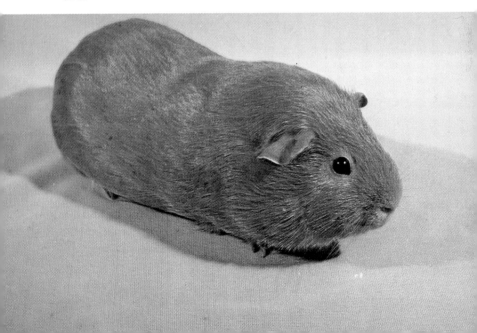

the body. Once it begins to squeak, continue to keep it warm, but do not give it anything to drink. After it has shown signs of life, you could fill a hot water bottle, cover it with a warm cloth and put your baby cavy either on or very close to the warm bottle. You could also cover the baby cavy.

When the baby is strong enough, usually about one and one-half hours after birth (you can tell it is strong because it will be standing up), give it back to its mother. Put the baby under her and watch if she will accept it; as she has not cleaned it, she will not know it.

As soon as the baby is born, the mother cavy starts to make encouraging sounds to it as she cleans and dries its body. At the same time she eats the membrane around it and disposes of the afterbirth. Sometimes the afterbirth is found lying in the hutch if the mother is weak after giving birth and cannot carry out her task. Other than slight blood stains on the bedding where the babies were born, the hutch is left in a very clean state. This is one reason why a litter of guinea pigs is not an unpleasant sight; one sees only the tiny babies, not a messy hutch.

As the mother continues to clean the new baby, it will stand and utter little cries. The baby will then snuggle under its mother and begin to suckle. Each new baby is treated in the same way when it is born. When all of the babies have arrived, each will nestle either under or around their mother. Often, after their bodies are dry, the mother will nudge each baby gently and call it into the corner of the hutch. There she will lie directly in front of her babies to keep them warm.

If you are breeding your cavies for showing, you will need to look for babies with exhibition potential. Gently press around the edges of the ears on the babies to take out any creases that are apparent. In exhibition stock, a crumpled ear is a fault, but if the creases are pressed out on the day that the babies are born, the ears will be perfectly shaped. Other than pressing the ears, you should not disturb the babies any further; just allow them to keep warm and to suckle. If you were to disturb them, they might rush around the hutch in fright. They sometimes get chilled when they move away from each other and chilling causes a setback in health.

A sow constantly cleans her babies by licking them. You will notice that when the babies are about a day or so old, they will rest on their backs or will nestle at the side of their mother. They will then raise their genital areas and their mother will continually lick these areas to induce them to pass urine and feces. Some dog breeds are reported to also do this. The absence of this stimulation is one of the causes of losses in hand-reared cavies.

The majority of sows treat their babies with devotion and care. You may notice, however, that your sow seems to be rejecting one of her babies. She may nudge it away from her, not allowing it to get under her for warmth or to suckle; the mother may even move to the opposite side of the cage and call the other young ones to join her. Instinctively a sow senses that something is wrong with a baby; it may be deformed, weak or blind. If a blind baby is allowed to live, it will go around in circles trying to find its mother. No matter how much you try to save the neglected baby, every time you place it with its mother, she will just leave and reject it.

Many exhibition stock owners practice what is known as "culling," humanely doing away with some babies from the litter on the day that it arrives. Culling keeps the owner from becoming over-stocked with cavies that are not up to exhibition standards. By leaving the sow with only two babies to nurse, the owner will raise cavies with extra stamina, since they will not have to share lactation with any other siblings. Culling seems to be a very cruel practice, but it is done in many animal hobbies.

A cavy is not a cannibal. Following the procedure of

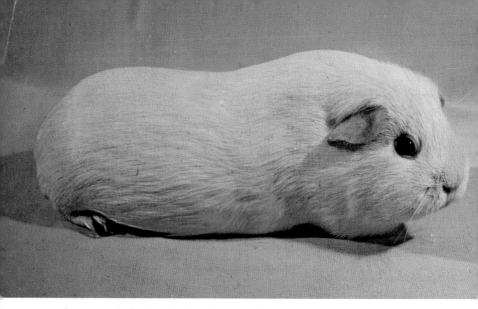

An even, delicate shade of cream, (like the cream of Jersey cows' milk) is the aim of fanciers as the ideal color of a Self Cream (or Creme).

A Self Cream Boar. Creams range in color from pale to dark cream. Photo by Brian Seed.

A Self Red Boar. Red is a vary attractive color, but it is subject to changes during a cavies' lifetime. A dark fiery red is the aim of breeders and not a dilute type of red.

Regardless of whether a long-haired cavy is kept as a pet or for showing, it has to be groomed regularly in order to keep the animal neat and comfortable. Photo by L. van der Meid.

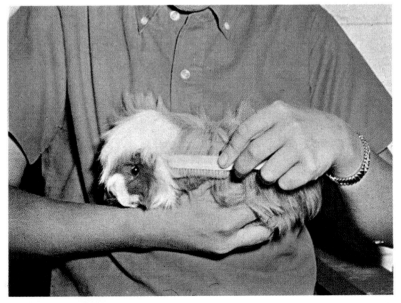

cleaning up after giving birth, she does not eat her young as many animals do. Sometimes a sow damages a baby's ear or its toe through earnest cleaning. In a difficult birth a baby sometimes gets mutilated as the mother grips it with her teeth in order to release it from her body.

NURSING

A sow has only two milk glands, each one situated at the base of the thighs. If the mother has more than two babies they have to take turns suckling. You must keep watch that the stronger babies do not push the smaller ones away and prevent them from suckling. If your sow does have a large litter and if there are weak ones, diluted milk can be given from a spoon (see "Hints on the Care of Motherless Baby

A White Abyssinian sow nursing one of her babies (brown colored) while two others wait their turn to suckle. Photo by L. Van der Meid.

Hay, when piled up like an igloo, can provide warmth and a feeling of security to a prospective mother. Photo by M. F. Roberts.

Cavies"). Bread and milk placed in a shallow dish is a good substitute. Soak the bread in boiling water, then drain it; add milk and cool. Do not give undiluted cow's milk—it is too concentrated and will sour quickly, giving the babies stomach upsets. It is better to use diluted canned evaporated milk.

If your sow has a litter of four or five babies, keep close watch on her condition. If she appears weakened by the time the babies are three weeks old, take the babies away from her because the lactation will be poor. With their continual suckling, the mother will utter little cries, as her teats are bitten and become very sore. If the babies are not taken away from her, her teats will reduce in size and be so damaged that future litters will have difficulty suckling. A weakened sow needs a long rest before being bred again.

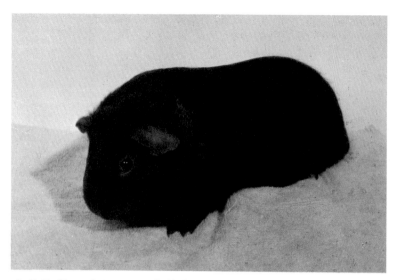

A Self Chocolate cavy. Self Chocolates are known to have the softest, silkiest coats among the Selfs.

A Self Chocolate sow.

Close-up of the eye region of a smooth-haired guinea pig. The eyes are susceptible to injuries from bedding (very dry hay, sharp wood chips, fine dust, etc.) and infections; they should be examined periodically.

A Peruvian should never have its hair held together by an elastic band.

FEEDING AND WEANING

The babies learn to eat solid foods rather quickly, because they are born with teeth. Your sow will take solid food and vegetables to where the babies sit huddled together and will teach them to eat. You can see them chewing on small pieces of bread, root, grass, vegetables, hay and dry foods when they are only twenty-four hours old. You should provide your sow with plenty of nourishing food, including vegetables, three times per day during the lactation period.

After your sow's babies are four days old, they will begin to grow very quickly and usually stay with their mother until they are about one month old. At this age remove the boars from their mother. The boars will be very virile at this point and will be capable of mating with their sister and mother; sows come into season any time after the age of one month. You can also remove any virile boars that cause any disturbance after the age of three weeks; they could be bitten on the ear and be ruined for exhibition.

The young females can stay with their mother until lactation has ceased. If you take the entire litter away from the mother all at once, always check the milk glands of the mother. If they are hard and swollen with milk, it is best to allow a few of the babies to suckle again to drain off the milk. If the milk is not drained she could develop an abscess or mastitis (inflammation of the milk glands). If your sow's glands are swollen and you have already given away the litter, take your sow off all green food for two days to prevent lactation; water, however, must be supplied.

When the litter has been weaned and if you are going to keep your younger sows, let them continue to live together, but you must separate the boars from each other after three months or you will have vicious fighting. At the end of the breeding season, select the well-grown young boars and sows that you will be using for the next season's breeding stock.

Hints on the Care
of Motherless Cavies

Many breeders of cavies face the problem of what to do with motherless babies. It will, of course, be a sad day for you when your sow dies and her babies survive, but it is important that you know how to face the problem.

FOSTER MOTHERS

Some owners do not wish to try to bring up motherless babies and they destroy the litter right away. However, some owners put the babies with a foster mother to see whether or not the sow will take them as her own. If you have a sow with young ones that are one or two days old, it is worth a try to see if she will accept the motherless babies.

You should take your foster mother out of her hutch and put her in a small box with proper bedding. If you leave her in the hutch she will keep roaming around and you will not be able to get the young ones to settle under her.

Once you have the sow in the box, take all but one of her own babies from her, and keep them warm. Before allowing the sow to see the newcomers, rub them against her own babies so that they will smell like them. You can then put the new ones with the sow; she will smell them after you have done this. If the babies are accepted, she will begin to clean them and make encouraging sounds. If she is going to reject them, she will put her nose under them and nudge them away from herself.

Wait to see if your sow will allow the babies to get under her to suckle, an hour should be enough time, and then re-

A group of guinea pigs with agouti color pattern. Although there is no known representative of the domestic cavy in the wild now, the agouti color pattern of the coat is still seen in some domestic strains.

A Silver Agouti boar. The belly of this breed has a narrow strip of gray hair without ticking.

A Golden Agouti boar. The undercoat is ticked with red, producing a deep mahogany or chestnut color. Photo by Brian Seed.

turn the rest of her own babies to her. Take all of them to her hutch where they will huddle together to keep warm and will take turns suckling.

If your sow rejects the new babies, and some do, it is worth your time and patience to try to save them yourself.

MANAGING AND FEEDING
MOTHERLESS CAVIES

The first thing you must provide is warmth. You can prepare a warm box for the babies by placing a hot water bottle inside a shoe box. Do not put the bottle on the bottom of the box; you have to refill it often to keep it warm and the babies will be disturbed when you pick them up to reach the hot water bottle. The bottle is more accessible if placed on the side of the box. You will need warm materials for the babies to sit on and to be covered with—old woolen scarves or socks will do nicely. You can also make an igloo from hay and put this in the corner of the box or cages; this would provide warmth as well as something on which the babies can nibble.

Once the babies are warm and stronger, you can give them a drink, canned evaporated milk diluted with warm water at the ratio of one part milk to three parts water. Undiluted cow's milk is too strong for the babies, as was previously mentioned.

To start the feeding, take one baby at a time and wrap it in a warm cloth. This will keep it warm and make it easier to hold. Feed a few drops of the milk mixture from a small tilted spoon, letting the baby suck it slowly. Do not lose patience and tip the milk down its throat because the liquid can go up its nose and down into the lungs, causing fatal milk pneumonia. Using an animal feeding bottle can have similar results.

Fed from a spoon, the babies will be very content. They will need milk about every one to two hours in the daytime for the first four days. If you give them a very late night

Most cavies, except possibly Peruvians and Shelties and pregnant sows, can withstand normal handling by children. Pregnant sows can lose their litters and the coats of longhairs can be ruined for showing through handling.

feeding and keep them very warm, they should be fine until the following morning. You may, if you wish, feed them during the night also. After each feeding, wash around their mouth with a clean, damp cloth and wipe off any milk that may have spilled on them. They are miserable if their coats are sticky. You must also wipe the anus and genital organs with a clean, damp cloth to induce the passing of feces and urine.

Baby cavies cannot live on milk alone and you will have to teach them to eat solid foods. Ordinarily it is the mother who teaches them to eat, but you can bring in one of your more mature young cavies to teach these babies to eat. Teaching baby cavies to eat is very difficult because they do not understand how to pick up food, but if the young cavy is gentle with them and eats the food that you provide, the babies will learn to eat by watching it. They can have hay, crushed oats, bread, tiny pieces of grass and some milk-and-bread mixture.

Breeding a perfectly marked Tortoiseshell and White cavy is very difficult. Ideally, the color patches should be clean-cut, clear and distinct, equally distributed and uniformly placed. The red must be deep, the white dazzling and the black jet. **Opposite:** Two Tortoise-shell and White cavies whose markings are of different dimensions and distribution. Photos by Brian Seed.

Until they are about ten days old, you should keep the babies inside your home where they will be easier to care for.

TERRIFIED MOTHERS

Sometimes a sow is terrified of her own babies, even though she has partially cleaned them. She will shriek and try to hide in the corner from them. When you try to place the babies close to her, she will appear frightened and will continue shrieking. The mother will not know what they are and the moving of these wet objects so close to her will continue to frighten her. If left in the hutch with her, the babies could die from being chilled.

The best thing for you to do when your sow reacts to her babies in this way is to put her in a small box and gently introduce her to her young, as if she is a foster mother. If they were born in an outdoor hutch, bring the mother and her babies inside your home to make it easier for you.

A good sow is generally protective of her young extending beyond the early stages after giving birth. Photo by L. van der Meid.

When a litter of young arrives it is advisable to remove members of an earlier litter, especially if the cage is small. Photo by L. van der Meid.

Hold the mother and let her smell each of her babies; then put her in the small box, even though she will probably continue to shriek. Begin putting the babies under her one by one. After awhile, she should sense what they are and begin to clean them and give them encouraging sounds as they try to huddle under her to suckle. Once she seems content with the babies, you can return the whole group to their hutch. Make sure she settles with them before feeding her, otherwise she will leave them again.

Should the mother not take to the babies, they still can be fed by one of your other sows. Any sow that is suckling a litter under ten days old can be used. You should sit down with a towel on your lap and hold the sow so that she is sitting on her rump, with her teats exposed. Hold a baby and put its mouth to the teats to let it suck from the sow. If you have difficulty in getting the baby to suck, you can make the milk flow from the teats by gently squeezing them; once the baby tastes the milk, it will begin sucking. If you are not certain that the baby is sucking, look closely at the side of its mouth where its hair will be moving when it swallows.

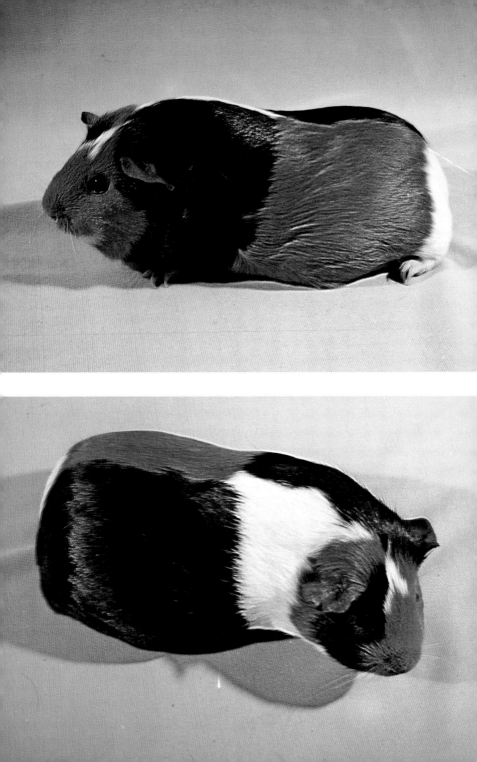

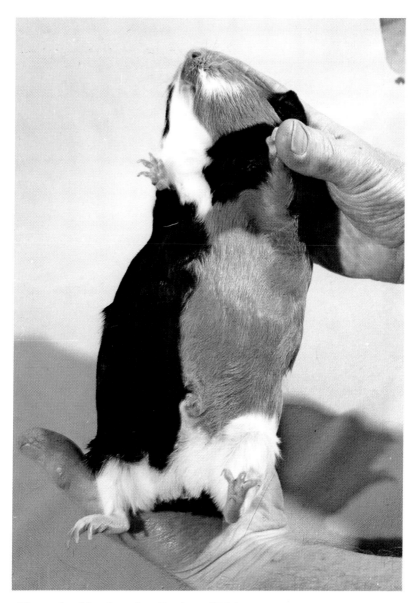

The underside of another Tortie and White cavy. The dividing line between the patches is not clean-cut, and a small patch of white hairs is present below the cheek. **Opposite:** The same cavy as seen from the side and the back. Photos by Ray Hanson.

Some cavy breeds that are popular in the United States: Peruvian, Abyssinian and Self. These breeds are available in many varieties also. Photo by Winston-Salem Journal Sentinel.

The Choice of Pure Breeds

Many breeders formed early attachments to the cavy as children, when they first had pet cavies. Their attachments grew and they later expanded their interests in the cavy to include breeding. People who keep a stud of cavies are known as "fanciers" and they refer to their cavies as "pigs"; we will be using those terms from this point on.

Before selecting stock to start your stud, you should get acquainted with a number of fanciers. If you do not know of any fanciers, go to your public library or nearest news stand and consult any literature that mentions cavy clubs or livestock societies. They should include helpful information about cavies, shows and stock purchasing. Many periodicals contain lists of clubs that specialize in certain stocks and you will be able to get the names of local or nearby fanciers. Some 4-H Clubs have projects on cavies, including showing, in their small animal programs.

Another suggestion, before selecting your stock, is that you visit a show where many different cavies are shown. When you talk to one fancier, he may rave about the particular breed that he has chosen and you will be convinced that that breed is the one that you want too. When you visit another show, after having already started your stud, you will see other breeds that will catch your eye and you will regret having made a hasty choice.

The popularity of a particular variety of pure breeds does not remain constant; what excels at one show will soon be forgotten as another breed takes home the awards at the next show.

New fanciers are always anxious to know how the judges make their decisions about variety choices at the shows and

A Tortie and White with markings of slightly different porportions, as seen from the right and left sides.

To a fastidious fancier these mismarked Dutch and Tortoiseshell and White cavies may be useless. but they are handsome animals and will make good pets.

A mixed collection of short-haired cavies of different colors and patterns. Mismarked animals are rejected by most fanciers. Photo by H. V. Lacey.

A pair of Dutch
cavies. Any self
color (except
cream and
white) or agouti
can be the
marking color
for a Dutch
guinea pig.

what the judges look for in a particular variety. To begin answering those questions, in this section we will discuss the Selfs, those cavies that are smooth-coated and all of one color.

THE SELFS

Selfs are bred in eight different colors in Great Britain: blacks, chocolate, red, cream, white, beige, golden and lilac. The British English Self Cavy Club gives a standard of excellence based on 100 points divided as follows:

Color For All English Self Cavies

Top Color – to be lustrous and of even
    shade all over the head and body.

Undercolor – to match top color down to
    the skin, giving an appearance free
    from flakiness. Hair on feet to match
    body color.   30

Type – broad Roman nose with a good width
    of muzzle, rounded at the nostrils,
    short and cobby body with very
    deep broad shoulders   25

Coat – to be short and silky with
    glossy sheen   15

Ears – rose petal shape, set wide apart
    large and drooping   10

Eyes – large and bold   10

Presentation – condition, cleanliness
    and grooming   10

    ————

    100

Together with the standard, detailed remarks are given for each color as follows:

Blacks – color should be deep and lustrous. Eyes, ears and pads black.

Whites – Should be pure snow white color. Eyes pink or black. Ears pink/white. Pads flesh pink.

Creams – Should be a pale even color, free from lemon

or yellow tinge. Eyes ruby. Ears pink/cream. Pads flesh pink.

Goldens – Should be a medium color with no suggestion of yellow, brassiness or redness. Eyes pink. Ears and pads pink/golden.

Reds – Should be a rich dark color. Eyes dark ruby. Ears and pads dark red/brown.

Chocolates – Should be a rich dark color. Eyes ruby. Ears and pads chocolate.

Beige – Should be an even medium color. Eyes pink. Ears and pads pink/beige.

Lilac – Should be an even medium dove grey color, with no suggestion of beige. Eyes pink. Ears and pads pink/lilac.

Faults:

Pronounced tufts on head and ruffles on belly to be penalized. Hairs of a different color to be penalized according to quantity. Breaks in coat to be penalized according to extent of damage. Wavy coats, mites attached to coat, dirty greasy or scurfy coats to be penalized according to the extent of the fault. Damaged or nibbled ears to be penalized according to the extent of the damage. Dark pigmentation of rims of ears to be penalized. No white toe nails except for whites. Missing toe nails. Additional toes. Nails on under 5 months and 5-8 months exhibits must not be cut. Sows in young should not be exhibited.

Side whiskers, fatty eyes, rosette(s), running lice in coat and breaks in skin are considered disqualifications.

Guidance to Judges and Exhibitors:

The outline of an English Self Cavy should consist of a gentle curve rising from the nostrils to the shoulders, then dipping to the back and levelling briefly before dipping once more over the hindquarters. Size to be very desirable but not at the expense of cobbyness or quality. Boars, if complying with the standard, shall not be penalized when in competition with sows.

A Black and White Dutch rabbit. In the United States the color standards for a Dutch rabbit and a Dutch cavy are the same. The British standard is not the same for both, however.

A Black Dutch cavy. Perfectly marked Dutch are difficult to find. The saddle is cut too far in this exhibit. Photo by Ray Hanson.

Above: A Dutch guinea pig that is held in a position so that the proper length of the stop is seen; the stops should be white and should be equal on the hind legs. Photo by Brian Seed. Below: Different color varieties of Dutch cavies on top of a carrying case, from foreground to rear: Golden Agouti, Red, Black, Chocolate and Silver Agouti. Photo by Brian Seed.

The American Cavy Breeders Association gives a standard of excellence for Selfs based on 100 points divided as follows:

Shape—broad shoulders, roman nose, body medium length, high full crown	25
Coat—short and silky	10
Ears—slightly drooping, not fallen, shapely, to match body	10
Eyes—large, bold, bright, to match body color	10
Feet—to match body color	5
Condition—firm flesh	10
Color—	30
	100

Remarks on the nine Selfs bred in the United States are listed below:

Beige—dark chamois color, deep and rich, with ears and feet to match; eyes pink

Black—deep rich black carries to base of skin; eyes black

Blues—dark rich blue carried to base of skin; eyes dark blue

Chocolate—deep rich and even, carried to base of skin; eyes dark with red cast

Cream—pure and even, free of brassy or lemon tinge, a delicate shade is required; eyes dark or ruby; ermissible

Lilac-pinkydove—same as lilac rabbit, allow for darker shades in juniors; eyes pink (or ruby)

Red-Eyed Orange—reddish orange, allow for darker shading in juniors; eyes ruby red

Red—deep rich red, allow for darker shading in juniors; eyes dark

White—pure even china white, free of brassy or lemon tinge; eyes pink

Week-old Self Black cavies in their carrying case (above). The same cavies held on the hand for closer view (below). Photo by B. Seed.

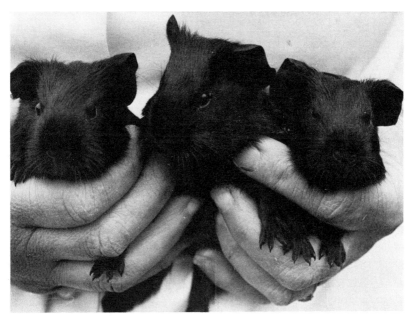

Cavy with three different colors in its coat. Unstandardized breeds are classified in some shows as rare varieties, but they can not compete with the standardized breeds.

A white-collared Golden cavy. A new variety is considered for standardization only after it has reached its greatest development and popularity. Photo by Harry V. Lacey.

Black Himalayan cavies. The points or dark markings on the extremities are not developed early. Notice that the nose marking, or smut, is still absent in the younger cavy.

A Black Himalayan cavy. Himalayans are born white; it takes about five months for the second color to develop fully. Photo by Ray Hanson.

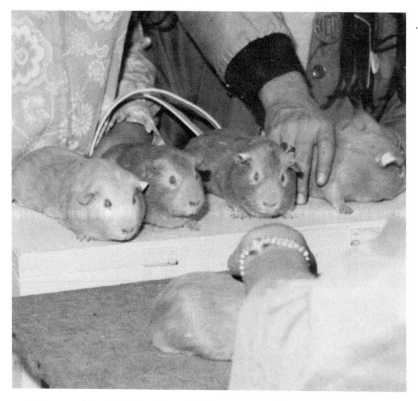

This quartet of light-colored Selfs on top of a carrying case are waiting their turn for being judged. Stewards help keep them in position, but they are expected to keep quiet during judging. Photo by B. Seed.

JUDGING SELFS

The judge must first place the cavy on a box on the judging table (boxes are not used in the U.S.) in order to see such qualities as shape or type, head, eyes, ear setting, shoulder and general appearance. If the cavy is held in the judge's hand, all of these points could not be judged properly. The cavy must then be held by the judge in his hand in the manner that was described in the earlier sections of this book. The judge will run his finger along the cavy's back, starting at the rump, turning the hair in reverse right up to the cheeks, to look for color that should continue right down to the skin. If the color is not continuous, the cavy will appear lighter and noticeably different. At this point the judge will look at the coat of a Black for any red or white hairs over the body, in the cheeks and around the vent—in these areas the lighter hairs sometimes appear in excessive amounts and the exhibit will be penalized. The judge then checks the chest and the stomach for colored hairs. Checking for color in Blacks is especially important because not all Blacks are of good body color. The Blacks' color plays an important part in the accumulation of points; it should be black with a greenish sheen. The judge will also look for good grooming; the toenails should not be too long and should be the right color.

The body should not be too long; if it is, it is referred to as being "long in the barrel." Narrow shoulders do not change with age.

The nose should not be too long from the eye to the tip of the nose, nor should the eyes be too close together. The eyes should not be sunken and dull but should be round and bold. The judge will take off points for the "fatty eye," an eye that looks like it has a ball of fat protruding from the side of the eyeball. The United States and British standards disqualify a cavy with this condition.

The judge will then look at the ears. Bad creases in the ears could have been prevented if they had been pressed out soon after the cavy was born. Some Self cavies have very bad carriage because the ears are short rather than drooping. Some have a black edging on the ear; this is a bad fault in the light colors. Torn edges on the ear are also a fault and must be penalized.

There can be deformities in the hair, usually hereditary in origin. Sometimes there is a triangular area of rough hair on the face between the nose and the eyes. The hair can be too long or form a skirt or cape around the hips and some have very long woolly coats. Another hair deformity is known as the "side whisker" which juts out from the side

Notice the developing points in these young pink-eyed Black Himalayans. Photo by David Whiteway.

A Black Himalayan cavy with a good smut; the smut must extend between the eyes and spread down to the whiskers. Photo by Brian Seed.

A Chocolate Himalayan cavy. The smut, ears and feet are of the same shade of chocolate milk brown. Photo by Brian Seed.

of the cheek like a tuft of twisted hair. All of these are faults of the smooth-coated Selfs and they should not be used for breeding purposes.

Often, the bone structure has been distorted in the very short-nosed Whites and Creams, and they will be heard wheezing and gurgling from the nose and the throat. This is a fault.

There are varying shades of Whites because some are bred from Creams. It is not advisable that you crossbreed Creams and Whites because the Creams bred in this way carry very light undercolor. Some Whites have a yellowish tinge in them and those that are not pure white are faulty. Creams range from very light to very dark, the dark being called "Buff." This color should only be used as a breeding stock to cross with a pale Cream so that the resulting offspring carry a better depth of color. With some very pale Creams, the stomach, chest and feet have a whitish tinge and so has the undercolor. These are all faults. Eye color must be watched in the Creams as some carry black eyes instead of the standard ruby eyes.

* The Golden Orange (Red-eyed Orange in the U.S.) was first introduced to the public in 1947 by the late Dr. W. M. Kerr and is the latest color to be presented in the Selfs. Many years ago the author had some of Dr. Kerr's cavies and now has some of the articles that he had written about them.

Golden Orange is a matter of controversy with judges because of their differing opinions about the meaning of a "rich golden shade." A class of Golden Orange varies from light to dark. The name suggests that the color should be rich and fiery, not a pale, washy color that carries poor undercolor. The nearest shade that several judges accept as the color can be seen in the color of the New Zealand Red rabbit, but even this differs from the color originally presented by the late Dr. Kerr.

---

* The Golden orange is now known as the Self Golden.

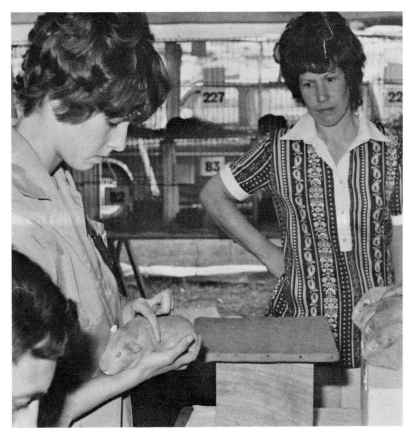

A judge in the process of examining a Self. To win, an exhibit must have qualities required by the Standard that are slightly better than others in its class. Photo by E. Jukes.

A fault with this color is that often the ears, feet pads, and skin around the eyes are sooty. Also, the toe nails are sometimes the wrong color. A sprinkling of white hairs along the sides can be found and often the feet are lighter in color and do not match the body color.

Faults found in the Self Chocolate again refer to varying shades. The standard reads "rich dark" but it can be seen that some are excessively dark, caused by the introduction of black to try to improve the shape (type) and depth of color. When the cavies are bred from Chocolate Himalayan di-

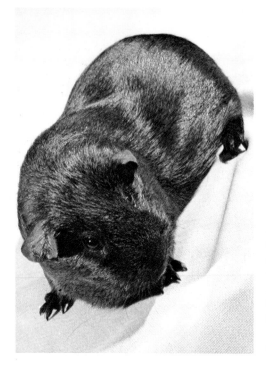

Left photo: Different shades of Golden Agouti are available for breeding a cavy with the desired shade of coat for showing. This specimen has a coat of deep blue-black hairs ticked with gold. **Lower photo:** A Silver Golden Agouti cavy. Features of the two most popular Agouti cavies, the Silver and the Golden, are present in this variety. Photo by Brian Seed.

A smooth Roan cavy. An even intermixing of black and white hairs occurs in the different parts of the body, except in the head and feet, which are black. Photo by Brian Seed.

A smooth Strawberry Roan cavy. Red and white hairs should be interspersed evenly, without patches of white or red hairs. Photo by Brian Seed.

lutes (like a pale-colored Chocolate Self cavy), the shade can not be called a true rich dark color. These produce some white young ones when crossed with a Self Chocolate. The young ones later turn into very poor pointed Chocolate Himalayans. The Chocolate, like the Cream, has the depth of undercolor reduced if it carries white factor.

A Chocolate can prove to be very disappointing when one of excellent color reaches the age of about five months. The baby coat will then be shed and the cavy will become speckled with cream hairs over the face and shoulders; some even get these hairs down their backs. Chocolates like this should not be kept for breeding stock. This speckling of colored hairs, however, does not appear in all Chocolates. The breakdown in color also appears in the Chocolate Dutch cavies.

Those that carry red hairs in small numbers should not be discarded but kept for breeding stock. This helps to improve the color of the Chocolate.

Judges who are not acquainted with the Self Chocolate can be overheard saying that they are "bare-skinned around the eyes and the nose." This is caused by their light skin pigment. On a closer look, the judge can see that the hairs in these parts are very fine and the lighter pigment shows through. They are not actually bare-skinned.

During the past few years the Self Red has deteriorated badly in shape or type. There are very few good colored Reds to be seen. Their beautiful mahogany color seems to be disappearing and is being replaced by a much lighter color. With the Self Red the eyes should be ruby; this is overlooked by many breeders and judges who accept black against the approved standard. When the Red carries black factor, the ears and feet pads will also be black.

The Self Beige is a pleasure to be seen when it has a very even top coat color, but a fault with this shade is that many are born with dark bars on the body and it takes a long time to see if they will clear when the cavy molts. Many never do

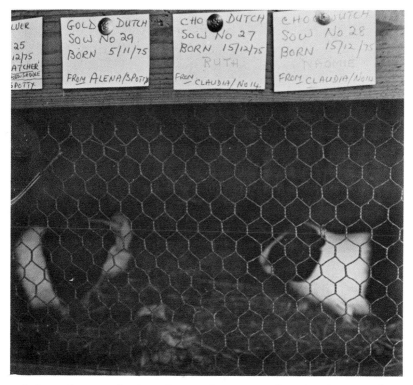

Information on the breeding performance of cavies is normally duplicated in the breeder's permanent breeding record book. Unless recorded, the data (shown here attached to the hutch) can be lost or destroyed. Photo by B. Seed.

clear. Often small patches of golden orange or red hairs will be found. When examining for undercolor, small spots of dark skin pigmentation can be found over the body. The Beige is also a controversial color, since it ranges from light to dark shades and different judges accept different shades. When the Beige was first introduced, its color was described as resembling the medium shade of the Champagne mouse which came in light, medium and dark shades. It was also written that the Beige was produced in hopes of breeding a Self that had a color resembling *cafe au lait*.

The Self Lilac is very close to the Self Beige, since both can appear in the same litter. The Lilac appeared in the ear-

The Dalmatian is a mutation from the Self Black; the body is white with black and gray spotting. Photo by David Whiteway.

A ridge-backed cavy. Showing is a good means of introducing a new mutation or a new variety to other fanciers and breeders. Photo by Brian Seed.

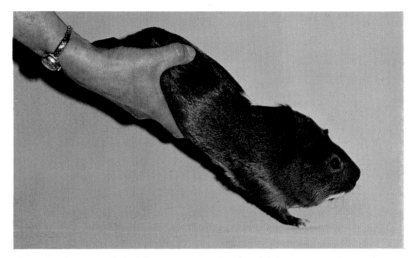

Incorrect way of holding a cavy. It should be grasped on the shoulders by one hand and supported on the lower rear end by the other hand. Photo by Mrs. I. Routledge.

A young Peruvian cavy.

ly days of the breeding of the Beige. Both the Lilac and the Beige carry similar faults of skin pigmentation on the body and the face, with dark edges to the ears. They can also carry some of the faults that appear in the other Selfs. Again, the color is controversial, the desired shade being a light pink hue as seen on the breast of a dove and not the very dark shade that resembles a slate roof.

When a judge looks at Selfs under five months of age, he must make certain allowances for color change. Golden Orange (Red-eyed Orange), Beige, Lilac and Red cavies are all born dark. During the first five months of their lives, the proper color appears first around the eyes, then the feet; it then spreads over the body until the baby coat has been molted completely. Thereafter, the full adult shade will be apparent.

NON-SELF VARIETIES

The non-self varieties may have ticked hair, markings set to a pattern, harsh rough or crested hair, inter-mixed colors or three varieties of long hair: Peruvian, Sheltie and Coronet. Compare each with photographs and study the standards.

AGOUTIS

The British standard for all Agoutis is:

Color—	20
Evenness of ticking throughout—	30
Shape—	20
Eyes—large and bold	5
Ears—well shaped and drooped	5
Size and quality—	5
Coat and condition—	15
	100

Remarks:

Goldens—The color should have a rich, deep golden hue throughout with even dark ticking, including the feet and the chest. The undercolor must be deep blue-black, carried well down to the skin. All four feet must be evenly ticked and free from any brassiness; feet which are too dark must be avoided. The belly color should be a rich gold, free from brassiness, and as narrow as possible.

Silvers—These should have a rich black undercolor with even silver throughout, including the chest and the feet. The belly color is a rich dark appearance and as narrow as possible.

Cinnamons—These should have a rich deep cinnamon undercolor with even and sparkling silver ticking throughout, including the chest and the feet; the belly color should have a rich dark appearance and be as narrow as possible.

Salmons—These should have a rich salmon color carried well down to the skin, should be silvered evenly all over, with a belly color of a self salmon.

Chocolate—These should have a rich deep cinnamon undercolor with light milk chocolate ticking. Ears and feet pads to be chocolate. Belly color to be of a lighter shade than the body color.

Lemon—These should have a blue/black undercolor with lemon ticking. Feet pads and ears to be of black pigment. Belly color to be a lighter shade than the body color.

Note—The following colors of Agoutis are the only ones recognized: Golden, Silver, Cinnamon, Salmon, Lemon and Chocolate.

Faults to be penalized—Eye circles, broken coat, side whiskers, excessive white hairs in the body, and odd feet.

Two long-haired cavies with different color patterns. The coat has to be groomed daily to prevent matting of the hair, especially in the area of the vent.

A long-haired, two-colored cavy. Matted hair is chewed, resulting in bald spots that can easily get infected and develop into sores.

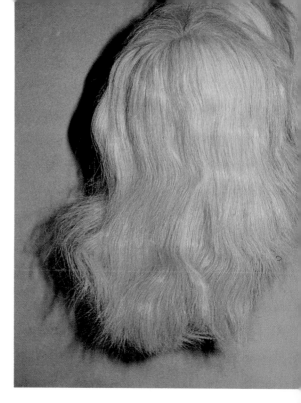

The backsweep of the Golden Peruvian measures about 22 inches long. The same cavy (below) is seen from the side. Its coat is so dense that the body is completely hidden. Photos by Mrs. I. Routledge.

In the American standard for the Agouti the 100 points are distributed as follows: 20 points for the shape; 10 points each for the eyes and feet; 5 points each for the coat, ears and feet; and 45 points for color.

The 45 points allotted for color are divided as follow:

Color –   15
Ticking –   30

An Agouti should have a body of moderate length, wide shoulders, a high full crown and a Roman nose. The coat must be silk-like and short; ticking must be uniformly distributed. The ears must match the body color and droop slightly but not fall. The eyes should be bright, alert, large and the same color as the body. The feet should be the same color as the body also. The cavy must have flesh that is firm, not flabby.

The following remarks apply to Agouti varieties exhibited in the United States:

Golden—A Golden Agouti should be of a rich, deep golden hue, with even, dark ticking all through, with chest and feet to match. The belly color should be a bright, dark red and as narrow as possible.

Silver—A Silver Agouti should be a bright silver hue, having even, dark ticking all through, with chest and feet to match. Chest and feet should be evenly ticked. The belly should be a bright white and as narrow as possible.

Cinnamon—A Cinnamon Agouti should be of cinnamon shade, having even ticking all through, with chest and feet to match. The belly color should be as clear yellow as possible and as narrow as possible.

All other colors—The belly color should be as near to top color as possible.

Faults to be penalized—Eye circles, muddy belly.

The importance in any color of Agouti is that the ticking should be evenly distributed throughout, except on the stomach. The stomach should not be ticked but should follow the standard for the various colors. The chest is a continuation of the sides and must be evenly ticked. Here, on the chest, there are often faults; at the sides of the mouth the ticking can be lost and result in light streaks, some of which run down onto the chest and are referred to as "bonnet strings." When the ticking has been lost around the eyes, there appears to be circles around them. If the cavy has a broken coat, the hair has been lost in small patches, disrupting the evenness of the ticking over the body. To check for any white hairs, run your finger from the rump end up to the head.

There is also great importance applied to the coloring of the feet. All four feet must be evenly ticked; faults arise by their being too dark from lack of ticking, or they can be excessively light. Highly selective breeding is necessary with Agoutis to get the desired feet ticking which must go down to the toes. An Agouti must be evenly groomed to show the beauty of the ticking and will be completely ruined if there are guard hairs jutting all over.

TORTOISESHELL

The standard for the Tortoiseshell in Britain is:

Patches—clear and distinct	45
Eyes—large and bold	10
Coat—	10
Size, shape and condition—	20
Color—black and red	15
	100

The points for the markings of the Tortoiseshell in the

Close-up of the face of a Peruvian cavy. The long stiff hairs around the nose and mouth are the whiskers.

A Tri-colored Peruvian boar. Photo by Mrs. I. Routledge.

A Bi-colored Peruvian cavy that is set up for showing. Photo by Ray Hanson.

American standard are distributed as follows:

Patches—as many well-defined dark red
and black patches as possible   25
Distribution—uniformly spaced and
equally distributed   <u>25</u>
         50

Remarks:

The color should be black and red as defined in the standard of the equivalently colored Self cavy (English or American) equally distributed in distinct patches; the smaller and more uniform the patches, the better. Small patch of white no larger than a British six penny piece or a U.S. dime is a fault, otherwise white patches are a disqualification.

Again, it is very difficult to breed the marked variety for their patches and very few are now seen. Those that are available carry good color, but some have brindling and unclear patches.

Tortoiseshell and White Abyssinians must be black, white and red, but not to a set pattern like the smooth Tortoiseshell and White.

TORTOISESHELL AND WHITE

The standard for all British Tortoiseshell and White:

Patches—clean cut, clear and distinct	25
Equal distribution and uniform placing of patches	25
Colors—black, red, white	20
Shape and size—	15
Eyes and ears—	5
Coat and condition—	10
	100

In the United States the point allocations for markings of the Tortoiseshell and White are:

Patches—	20
Distribution—	30
	50

The color to be Black, Red and White, in 3 square cut patches of equal size and placed alternately on each side of the cavy. Each color must be clear and distinct without being intermixed one with another.

Faults:

Side whiskers, bands and belts are faults. Cavies being short of any colored patch on either side shall be penalized.

The standard for the Tortoiseshell and White cavy requires that there should be three colors—black, red and white—on both sides in square patches that are as alike as possible. The dividing line runs down the center of the back from the nose, between the ears, down to the rump and then goes underneath and in-between the hind legs along the belly to the middle of the chin. On each side of this line the colors should be alternating. If any color should run over the line and go part of the way around the body, it is a belt and around the body it is a band. Brindling

111

The first steps in wrapping the sweep of a Peruvian are shown in these photos taken by Mrs. I. Routledge.

After wrapping, the sweep is completed as seen above. It is then secured by a rubberband as shown below. The same method is used for wrapping the sides. Photo by Mrs. I. Routledge.

Compare this Abyssinian with the standard for rosettes, ridges, head furnishings and mane. Photo by Eric Jukes.

occurs when hairs are intermixed in the patches. An exhibit in the United States would lose points on the same faults also.

The Tortoiseshell and White cavy is a marked variety, so you need great patience and skill to breed them. So few are suitable for exhibition. It is a striking variety, with its beautiful colors and clear-cut patches. One fault that arises is brindling, intermingling of red and black colors. This should be avoided, if at all possible; it is not desirable as breeding stock as the aim is for clear-cut and distinct patches. Two colors on a side instead of three or more is also a fault. Good color must be maintained. Belts or bands of color that go partly around the body are faults. The head should be divided in colors rather than being of one solid color. While a good dividing line can be achieved on the stomach, it is very difficult to breed one down the back.

BI-COLOR AND TRI-COLOR

The Bi-Color and Tri-Color are marked cavies with any two or three colors. The Bi-Color is marked in the same way as the Tortoiseshell.

The British standard for the Tri-Color is:

Patches – clear and distinct	45
Eyes – large and bold	10
Coat –	10
Size, shape, condition –	20
Color – any three colors	15
	100

Remarks:

Colors to be any two or three colors as defined in the British English Self Cavy Club standard or Agouti Cavy Club standard. Brindling and banding are faults.

Tricolors are bred in colors other than red, black, and white. They are bred on similar lines to the Tortoiseshell and White and have the same faultings. Again, being a marked variety, it is exceedingly difficult to breed to exhibition standard, so it is well worth showing any that have reasonably clear-cut patches with little brindling.

In the United States the Bi-color and Tri-Color are included in the Broken Color class of the marked cavies. Broken Color includes cavies of any two or more colors, excluding the Tortoiseshell, Tortoiseshell and White, Himalayan and Dutch marked cavies.

Point allocations for Broken Color are as follows:
Patches – as well-defined and clear as possible: 25 points. Distribution – uniformly positioned and evenly distributed: 25 points. Total: 50 points.

With its long hair washed and brushed earlier, this Sheltie is now ready for wrapping. Photo by Mrs. I. Routledge.

A piece of common wrapping paper (others use cloth) is used to wrap the sweep. Photo by Mrs. I. Routledge.

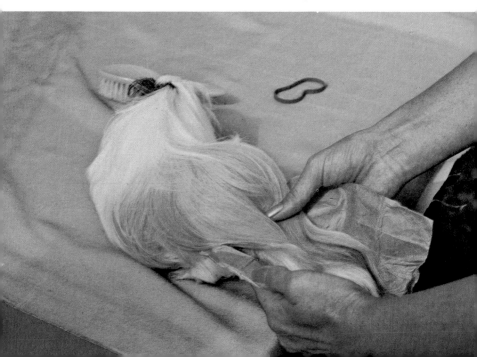

After the sweep is fully enclosed in the paper, the bundle is folded, accordion-like, and then it is secured with a rubber band. Photo by Mrs. I. Routledge.

From January 1980 the Crested Sheltie is now known as the Coronet. A rosette is present on the top of the head, otherwise it is a typical Silky or Sheltie. Photo by Ray Hanson.

The remaining 50 points are allotted to the general appearance and divided as follows:

Shape—	15
Coat—	10
Eyes—	5
Condition—	10
Color—	10
	50

Dutch-marked, Himalayan, Tortoiseshell, and Tortoiseshell and White cavies are eliminated from competing.

DUTCH

The British standard for the Dutch is:

Blaze and cheeks—	15
Clean neck—	10
Saddle—	10
Undercut—	10
Feet stops—	15
Ears—	15
Eyes—	5
Color—	10
Size, Shape, Condition—	10
	100

In American shows the Dutch cavy is judged according to the following standard worth 50 points for its markings (50 points are alloted to general appearance):

Cheeks—	12
Blaze—	5
Saddle—	10
Undercut—	8
Neck—	5
Stops—	10
	50

Remarks:

The cheek markings should be round; they should not include the smellers but should come as near to them as

A well marked Dutch cavy boar. Its saddle is straight and the cheek blaze does not encroach on the nostril. Photos by A. S. W. Elward.

possible without touching. The feet stops must not go around the hocks. The ears should be sound and of the same color as that of the body. Any flesh marks will lose points. Any rough hair or rosettes will lose ten points.

The colors of the Dutch are red, black, golden agouti, silver agouti, chocolate and cream.

According to the American standards, markings of the Dutch cavy should be placed like they are in the Dutch rabbit. Dutch rabbit disqualifications are applicable to Dutch cavies as well.

The Dutch, like any other of the marked varieties, should only be a breed of choice. Fanciers need to have great patience with these as untold disappointments arise with the breeding of this variety.

The Dutch is one of the author's favorites and she has kept them for very many years. All present-day Chocolate Dutch have in some way originated from this stud, since after World War II the author was the only known breeder left with this color. About twenty-four years ago great in-

Top view of a dark Tri-colored Peruvian sow. The head furnishing or frontal fringe, the sidesweeps, and backsweep are balanced in their lengths. Photo by Mrs. L. Routledge.

Opposite, upper photo: A good Peruvian must have a frontal fringe that covers the head completely. Many otherwise good Peruvians lose points because the frontal fringe is missing or sparse. **Opposite, lower photo:** Top view of a dark Peruvian boar. Infestation with lice can ruin Peruvians. When irritated by louse bites, they will scratch out the hair. Photos by Mrs. L. Routledge.

terest was caused when the author exhibited a Chocolate Dutch because it was believed that the variety was extinct. According to published articles it was freely exhibited in the early part of this century.

The Dutch cavy's markings with any of the colors named has a set pattern with a white background, similar to the Dutch rabbit. The cavy has never been able to make the progress with its markings that the rabbit has. It is far more difficult to breed a cavy to the required standard.

Outstanding Dutch cavies have been bred and have won the Best in Show award, but the majority of those that are exhibited still have a number of faults in relation to the standard. The aim is for well-balanced markings, with cheeks and feet stops being as even as possible. The feet stops are allowed to be uneven when exhibited, owing to the difficulty in breeding a well balanced Dutch. These stops are the white markings which include the toes and extend along the foot for a desired length of one-half of an inch. Stops must not go around the hock or heel.

The foot pads must be examined; often the stops may be the correct length on the top of the foot, but white skin will run to the hock, where the skin should be the main body color. It is a fault if a stop of correct length and skin color has a line of fine white hairs leading to the hock on the inside of the foot. A Dutch with only one stop is unsuitable for exhibition, no matter how fine its markings may be otherwise. Such a cavy can only be used for breeding stock.

The saddle, which should be across the body in the main color, should be nearer to the shoulders. A high-cut saddle is better than one that cuts back toward the hips; this latter type looks as though the saddle is slipping off the rump. When the saddle is not straight across the body it is referred to as being skewed and is faulted. The saddle should continue in a straight line around the body with the part under the stomach as the undercut; often this undercut has a dip or a "V" in the center and is a fault.

The standard stipulates that a Dutch cavy should have a straight saddle with blaze and cheeks of the correct shape. Feet stops are also missing in this specimen. Photo by M.F. Roberts.

The blaze (head marking on a Dutch) should be wedge-shaped and tapering off finely; often this is too wide or narrow. Ears should not have a flesh marking, meaning flesh-colored skin instead of being the color of the body.

It is wrong to judge a Dutch cavy while holding it in the hands. This can cause distortion to the markings by stretching the skin, giving a false impression of the exhibit. A Dutch should be held in the hands only for examining color, condition and foot pads—other than that it should be on the judging table, with the judge's hand over the head of the cavy and his finger and thumb under the jaws. The head and front part should be lifted up so that the judge can see if the cheeks are odd. With the cavy's back feet remaining on the judging table, the judge can correctly examine the undercut. The saddle must be observed from above, giving the best possible view of the saddle's position. The head should be checked for any drags, such as the main color jutting out from the rounded cheeks. When looking down on the blaze, the judge can see if the cheeks are even there.

Very many Dutch cavies have to be bred before one is found suitable for exhibition.

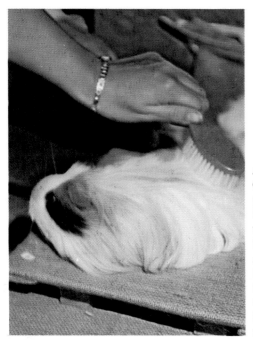

A Silky (Sheltie in Great Britain) in the process of being brushed. Unlike Peruvians, Shelties lack a frontal fringe. **Below:** A wrapping should be light and comfortable, or else the cavy will chew it off. Photos by Ray Hanson.

A Sheltie with an impressive display of awards (plaques, cups, rosettes) it has won for its owner.

HIMALAYAN

The standard for the Himalayan is:

Nose—even and jet-black or chocolate	25
Feet—jet-black or chocolate	20
Ears—shapely and jet-black or chocolate	10
Coat and color—short, silky, pure white	20
Shape and size—	10
Eyes—large, bold, ruby red	5
Condition—	10
	100

The American standard for Himalayan marking is the following:

Nose—	15
Feet—	10
Ears—	10
Density of markings—	15
	50

Remarks:

These should have a black or chocolate nose, feet, and ears. Nose markings should be well carried up to the eyes. The body should be pure white. The eyes are ruby red, deep pink.

Any Black that has excessively poor body color is to be severely penalized.

Any Chocolate with excessively poor body color and/or excessively dark points is to be severely penalized.

Disqualifications are based on any white toenails and/or white patches on the foot pads.

The Himalayan is another of the marked variety and is bred in either black or chocolate. This cavy has markings similar to the Himalayan rabbit but does not generally carry such dense points or pure white body color as the rabbit.

Points should be either black or rich chocolate in color; points refer to color markings of the ears, feet and nose, that of the last often called the "smut."

Generally, you can easily see when the cavies are born whether or not they have exhibition potential by observing their set patterns and markings. This is where the practice of culling plays an important role if you plan to keep only those cavies that are suitable for exhibition. This is not so easy with the Himalayans. They are born pure white and their markings gradually appear. By the time they are five months old, you can make a better assessment of their potential for exhibition. The points will show their density, but some white hairs in these should still be left to molt out. This is not considered to be a fault in a cavy that is under five months old; it shows that it is an exhibit of correct age.

Should the white body color change to a sepia hue (smutty brownish), it will be faulted for not having the pure white body color. The feet must all be black and matching. They will be faulted if they have poor density, or are brindled or speckled with the sepia hue on the back feet; the front feet could be a little better on density.

The ears must be black to match the other points. The nose point or smut often fails on size and on density. This should be egg-shaped and the tapering end should go well up between the eyes and be black in color. Often the smut is like the feet, speckled or brindled, and has to be faulted.

The Chocolate Himalayan is judged in the exact same way as the Black, the difference being that the ears, feet and nose will be a rich milk chocolate color with a white body.

The Chocolate Himalayan dilute is bred by mating a Self Chocolate with a Chocolate Himalayan. Of this mating some of the young ones would resemble a light-colored Self Chocolate. These should be used for Himalayan breeding to try to improve density in the chocolate color of the

One of the new breeds of Sheltie displayed on a grooming board. Note the beautiful color and excellent condition of the sweeps.

Although silvering is normally caused by a certain gene, scientists have also been able to produce the same effect by the action of three other types of genes together.

A cavy is an ideal pet for children. Cavies are clean, docile and easy to care for; they also live fairly long, more than four years.

points. These light-colored Chocolates should not be exhibited as Self Chocolate cavies.

The two colors in the Himalayans can be exhibited in the same class; and at times when density is poor in the Blacks, they can be mistaken for a Chocolate. In order to make a decision, look at the ears and the feet pads; if the cavy is Black, these will also be black. The Chocolate has brown feet pads and ears.

Often when an exhibit has purity of the body color, it may fail on the points, or *vice versa*. Like all marked varieties, the Himalayan is not an easy cavy to breed for exhibition, as climatic conditions or even a knocked foot on the feeding dish will cause density to decrease. Additionally, it should not be housed in the sunlight as this tends to darken the body color.

BRINDLES

The standard for all Brindles:

Even intermixing of colors—	45
Eyes—large	10
Coat—	10
Size, shape, condition—	20
Color—intermixed black and red	15
	100

Brindles judged in an American exhibit receive a maximum of 45 points for color distributed as follows:

Intermixture of black and red: 10 points. Even mixture of colors: 35 points. Total: 45 points.

Remarks:

The color should be black and red (as defined in the corresponding Self standard), intermixed evenly all over the head, body and feet, with black and red hairs in equal proportions.

This is one of the lesser seen varieties owing to the difficulty breeding them with intermixed colors. The are inclined to have patches of solid color of either red or black and they are faulted for this.

ROAN

The standard for the Roan is:

Roan—Mixing to be even throughout	30
Head—Clean cut and solid black	10
Feet—Solid black	10
Eyes—Black, large and bold	10
Coat—To be short and silky, black and white	10
Ears—Black, set wide apart, large and drooping	10
Size, type and condition	20
	100

Disqualifications—Fatty eye, side whiskers.

Colored Roans—All colored roans must conform to the respective coat color requirements set down by the British English Self Cavy Club or in the case of Agoutis the British National Agouti Cavy Club.

The Roans shown in the United States will receive at best a total of 45 points for color:

Intermixture of colors: 15 points. Even distribution of roaning: 30 points. Total: 45 points.

The roan is basically a black cavy with white hairs evenly intermixed throughout the body. Solid black should be confined to the head and feet, but white whiskers should not be penalized. Odd colored hairs, patches of black or white on the body and poor demarcation between the head and body should be penalized. The type and overall shape of the roan, should ideally conform to the requirements of the Self cavy. Eye color is black but in certain lights this may appear to be ruby, this is not a fault.

This is a rather striking cavy, with its solid black head and feet and with white hairs intermixed on its body. The intermixing of white hairs can form small white spots and the cavy will be faulted when this occurs. It is also a fault when the belly is a shade too light, or when black is excessive all over the body; the cavy will be too dark. There must be a demarcation between the black and the roaning; where this appears as a jagged edge, the cavy will be faulted.

A Tortoiseshell and White Abyssinian cavy. Photo by Brian Seed.

A Blue Roan Abyssinian cavy. Photo by Brian Seed.

Abyssinian boars make better show animals because they have harsher coats than sows. Rosettes tend to flatten if the hairs are soft. Photo by Harry V. Lacey.

A Tri-colored Abyssinian cavy. Photo by Harry V. Lacey.

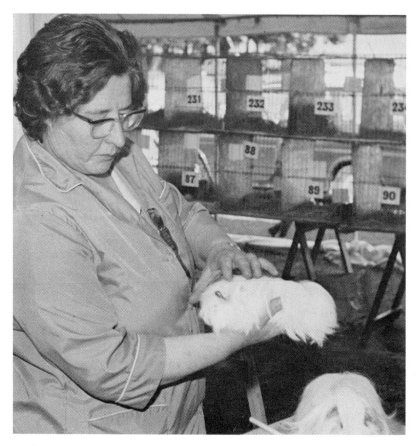

The critic—Miss T. Redeglia in the process of examining the coat of a Peruvian during a pen show in England. Note the many holding pens in the background on top of temporary tables. Photo by E. Jukes.

American cavy clubs recognize, in addition to the Blue Roan (black and white), two other Roan varieties: Strawberry Roan (red and white) and Tri-Color Roan (combination of black, red and white). Most roans have solid colored heads, with the roaning starting around the shoulders. Patches of solid color on the body are allowed, but they should be clearly defined. Everything being equal, the one with the least number of solid patches will be preferred. Eyes are dark.

PERUVIAN

The standard for the Peruvian is:

Head—broad, with prominent eyes	5
Fringe—the hair completely covering the face	15
Shoulders and sides—	15
Texture—silky	20
Density—	15
Sweep, length of fullness, the hair flowing over the hindquarters	15
Condition—	5
Size—	5
Presentation—	5
	100

The American standard for Peruvians is as follows:

Appearance (general)—	5
Coat density—thick	13
Coat texture—silk-like and soft	13
Rear sweep—long, even to side sweeps	13
Side sweep—long, even to rear sweep and frontal fringe	13
Frontal fringe—like a thick mane, falls fully over head and shoulders	13
Color—same eye and coat color; both match corresponding American variety	10
Condition—clear, shining coat; firm flesh	10
Type—alert and unclouded eyes, wide shoulders, moderate length	10
	100

Remarks:

The hair should be fine, silky and glossy; the fringe or head furnishing should fall well over the nose. The shoulders should be so furnished with hair that the hair hangs in a thick mane on each side of the head. The face should be short and the eyes should be large and full. While we aim for a straight coat, a slight wave should not be unduly penalized. If the sweep (the hair from the hindquarters) is slight-

135

An American Crested cavy. In this breed the contrasting hair color should be confined to the crest, or "star," as some geneticists call it. Photo by Brian Seed.

An American Crested Golden cavy. Photo by Ray Hanson.

An all-white Crested cavy. Photo by Ray Hanson.

Ideally, the mid-dorsal part of a long-haired variety should be straight. This is a genetic factor, but grooming can help a little to keep some misaligned hairs in place. Photo by M. F. Roberts.

ly longer than the side sweeps. This does not constitute uneven length.

During the judging, the Peruvian is judged with its long silky hair brushed out. It is first examined on a stool (nine inches high and not more than sixteen inches in circumference) that is covered with burlap. The Peruvian, sitting on the stool, is then placed on the judging table. In American shows the Peruvian is examined on a wooden box (18 inches square and 4 inches high) covered with burlap. Slots on two opposite sides make lifting the box easier.

An assessment must be made of the hair, its thickness and texture, its coarseness or fineness. The sides should not be thin or uneven and the sweep not thin and straggly. The ends of the hair from the sides and sweep will not be as dense as that of the body since the long hair is the top coat which protects the shorter undercoat.

The face is covered with hair coming from behind and between the ears; this is called the "fringe" or the "frontal." In an adult, this hair should touch the surface of whatever the cavy is sitting on. If the hair does not touch, the cavy will be faulted for having hair that is too short. Since the face is covered, a check is made to see if the cavy has two sighted eyes; it could be blind which is also a fault. The judge then lifts the cavy onto either hand, as instructed in the chapter on the handling of the cavy. He checks to see that the hair hanging down contains no gaps, tangles, mats or signs of having been cut where it might have become soiled and slightly matted.

From this manner of holding the cavy, evenness can also be observed. This variety should be treated with care on the judging table and during any handling; it should not be turned almost upside down for examination. By such rough treatment the nails of the back feet could get caught in the hair, pulling out a section and completely ruining it for further exhibition.

Often what resembles gaps in the hair close against the skin is nothing more than the dividing line where the hair goes into wrappers. This is not a fault.

SHELTIE

The standard for the Sheltie is:

Head – broad with short nose and large, prominent eyes; with hair lying towards the rump; Ears petal shape, set slightly drooping with good width between.	15
Mane – sweeping back to join with sweep and is not parted.	15
Shoulders – Broad with hair of a good length and density continuing evenly around sides.	20
Coat – Silky texture and good density.	20
Sweep – Length and fullness of hair falling over hindquarters (sweep generally to be longer than the sides which should be even in length)	20
Condition and presentation – to be presented with no parting.	10
	100

A pair of English Crested cavies.

The position of the crest (a single rosette) is strictly specified by the standard: it can not be farther forward than the posterior of the eye nor farther back than the front of the ear. Photo by Brian Seed.

Back view of a Dalmatian cavy. Dalmatians are bred in other colors besides black. Photo be David Whiteway.

The American standard for the Silky (Sheltie to British fanciers) is:

Head—short, broad Roman nose, eyes large and bold, ears slightly drooping	10
Body—medium length, broad shoulders, full crown	10
Coat—soft and silky texture	10
Density of coat—very dense	13
Sweep—mane, long hair; sweep to join rear sweep, not parting, uniform length	13
Side sweep—long, uniform, balanced with rear sweep	13
Rear sweep—full, long and uniform, may be slightly longer than the side sweep	13
Condition—firm flesh, bright coat	10
Color—to match American description, including eyes	8
	100

Remarks:

The mane should sweep back from the forehead, fall behind the ears, over the shoulders, along the back and merge with the sweep. The sweep is generally longer than the sides. The sides are even in length. There should be no part along the back.

The Sheltie (or Silky in the U.S.) is the other variety that has long hair; you can easily see that it does not resemble a Peruvian because the head furnishing is so different. Study the photograph and you will notice that the face is smooth-coated. No hair at all is allowed to fall over the face like a fringe or a frontal (head furnishings). It must have a broad head and a short nose (similar to the shape required in the Self cavy), with bold eyes. The hair known as the mane should fall towards the rump, joining with the rear sweep.

It does not have a parting down the middle of the back. The shoulders are important; they must be broad and the hair on them should be slightly longer with good density, continuing along the sides of the cavy at equal lengths. Faults arise on the shoulders where the hair is sometimes thin and short. The long hair should begin past the cheeks but with this shoulder fault, the long hair begins beyond the front legs giving a racy appearance.

The rear sweep, which is generally longer than the side sweeps are, must be even in length and have good texture and density. It would be a fault if the hair anywhere on the body looked thin, uneven, or straggly or if there were any gaps where hair had been cut to remove mats.

The presentation and examination of the Sheltie or Silky for judging is done in the same way it is done for the Peruvian.

ABYSSINIAN

The standard for the Abyssinian is:

Rosettes—	20
Ridges—	20
Coat—	20
Shape and size—	10
Head furnishings and mane—	15
Color—	5
Eyes and ears—	5
Condition—	5
	100

The American point distribution for the Abyssinian standard is slightly different from that of the British:

Rosettes –	25
Coat –	20
Shape –	15
Head –	10
Eyes –	5
Condition –	10
Color/Markings –	15
	100

A marked boar and its offspring. Their blazes are similar, but the black markings are diminished in the younger animal.

A trio of cavies from Germany: a Silver Gray, a Piebald of tan and white (called Isabella in Europe) and a Tri-colored with tufted ears.

Pink eye is an independently inherited character, so it is possible to breed this trait in other varieties. However, it can have a diluting effect on certain coat colors.

Remarks:

Rosettes should be well formed and radiate from a clearly defined center. They should be placed as follows: four rosettes around the hindquarters, four in a direct line across the body and one or two on each shoulder. Each rosette should be clear and distinct from any other. The coat should be rough, erect, and wiry and should not exceed one and one-half inches in length. In shape and size it should be cobby, thick-set, broad at the shoulders, have a good scruf and large throughout. The head should be well furnished with hair and have a good moustache. The mane is erect, harsh and wiry with a ridge extending from it in an unbroken line down the middle of the back to the ridge that is formed by the hindquarter rosettes. The colors should be clear and bright with plenty of luster. The eyes should be large and bold; the ears should have a nice drooping to them. The coat is close and thick, the flesh firm and hard

The ridges and rosettes in this Abyssinian are not well defined. Photo by L. van der Meid.

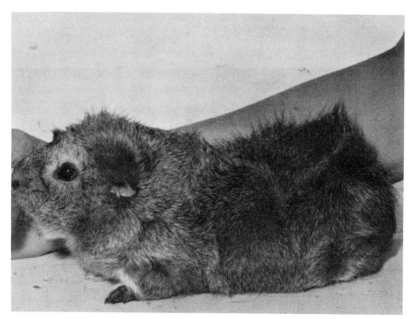

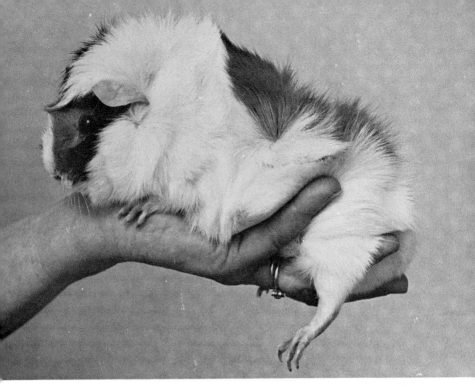

An Abyssinian is not held on the hand while being judged for its coat, but is allowed to walk on the judging table instead. Photo by B. Seed.

when handled. Flatness anywhere is a fault, especially on the back; double, split, flat or open-center rosettes are also faults.

The Abyssinian is the only variety that has a harsh, wiry, and rosetted coat. It is a very attractive animal and is bred in various colors.

In the Tortoiseshell and White color (red/black/white), the Tortoiseshell is in red and black patches which should be as clear as possible. Brindles can be either light or dark colored, meaning that the red and black are intermixed. If the red hairs predominate it is a light Brindle; if the black hairs predominate it is a dark Brindle. Occasionally, a Brindle or Tortoiseshell may have a small patch of white hairs on it. If the white-haired area does not exceed the size of a

The Abysinnian's rough coat is a dominant trait over the normal hair, but another set of modifying factors determines the position of the whorl. Color is inherited completely independently from coat texture.

Opposite, upper photo: If this parent cavy is indeed the parent of these young cavies, it must be a hybrid that was mated to another hybrid or to an albino in order to produce some albino offspring. **Opposite, lower photo:** Cream is a recessive trait, but this cavy parent has colored young; color must have originated from the other parent.

149

Unlike a Self, harsh not soft hair, is required in an Abyssinian exhibit. Photo by Dr. H. R. Axelrod.

British pence piece (about the size of an American quarter) it can be exhibited in its classified color class.

Self-colored Abyssinians must not become confused with the smooth-coated Self Cavy; its rosetted coat defines it. The colors usually seen are black, red and white, but on occasion, other self colors can be seen.

There are also the Abyssinians that come under the heading of "Off Color Varieties." This includes the Blue Roan, which is slate gray intermixed with white hairs, and the Strawberry Roan, which has red hairs intermixed with white hairs. Other Abyssinians are red and white, black and white, agouti, Himalayan, and some other colors; they can always be recognized by their harsh, rough coats and rosettes.

The Abyssinian is judged differently from any other breed. It must be allowed to walk on the judging table, where it can show off its good and bad points, according to the standard. Held in the hands, there could be a distortion of the rosettes and the ridges. They should be handled only for examination of minor points.

What does the judge look for in an Abyssinian? As the standard states, it must have well-formed rosettes. These should be cone-shaped and there should be four in a direct line across the body, four around the hindquarters and one or two on each shoulder. Each rosette should be clear and distinct from the other.

The rump rosettes should radiate from a pinpoint but should be thumb-shaped so that the top of the rosettes joins the back ridge. Faults arise here when the rump rosettes are placed too low; as the cavy walks on the table, the back ridge will lie flat instead of being erect. It is also a fault to have what is called a "guttering of the hair," where a line appears running through the rosettes.

The ridges are very important; it must be remembered that the higher the ridges, the deeper the rosettes. The

A crossbred Abyssinian, obvious by the long rosetted hair. Photo by Dr. H. R. Axelrod.

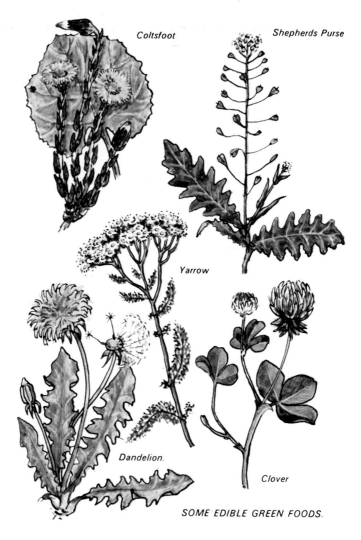

Coltsfoot

Shepherds Purse

Yarrow

Dandelion.

Clover

SOME EDIBLE GREEN FOODS.

Some edible green foods.

Foxglove

Lily of the Valley

Convolvulus

Deadly Nightshade.

Buttercup

SOME POISONOUS PLANTS.

Some poisonous plants.

center ridge starts from the head and ends at the back ridge.

When the saddle rosettes are in line and the hair erect, the back ridge should be straight. This ridge runs across the rump and behind the saddle rosettes and is parallel to the collar ridge. The collar ridge runs down from the shoulders or midway between the head and saddle rosettes. It is a fault when the collar ridge is flat; it should be erect like the back ridge, which is formed by the hair from the hip and rump rosettes.

The hair must be harsh and wiry. If the hair is short, it causes flatness over the body; *any* such flatness is a fault. Other faults are bare-centered rosettes, double and split rosettes, short hair and soft coat.

At the age of two to three months, an Abyssinian still has its soft coat. Since the coat does not change to harsh hair at molting until it is four months old, it is not a good idea to show such a very young Abyssinian.

The head must be well-furnished with hair and have a good moustache. A mane leaning to one side instead of being erect is faulted. The ears must droop.

If an Abyssinian's body is long instead of cobby, the collar and back ridges will be too far apart, spoiling the saddle rosettes' shape.

The general belief is that the breeding stock must carry the desired coat harshness. Some fanciers feel that keeping Abyssinians under cool condition (*e.g.,* outdoors) helps achieve this. Naturally, summer heat affects cavy hair, but as cooler weather approaches the correct hair texture should return.

TEDDY

In the United States there is a second variety of coarse-haired cavy exhibited. The breed is new and placed under a provisional standard. It is called Teddy. Initially this mutation is known in Tortoiseshell and White only. The coat is close, short and thick, and coarse and harsh in texture; the hair shafts are "kinky." Ridges and rosettes are absent. Because it is a new variety a slight center part, a soft coat and erect ears on a slightly pointed head are allowed. The standard is expected to be more definite when the breed is finally accepted.

The provisional standard for the Teddy is:

Shape—	15
Coat—(Texture: 15; Length: 10; Density: 5)	30
Head—	10
Ears—	5
Eyes—	5
Condition—	10
Color—	25
	100

The British version of the Teddy is the Rex. A few are seen at the Rare Varieties Stock Shows. They do not have a standard, but the United States provisional standard is quoted in British periodicals.

DALMATIAN
British standard for the Dalmatian is given below:

Spotting—Black spotting on white body, clear and distinct, well distributed over body.	30
Head—White blaze with black either side. Shape of head to be broad with Roman nose.	20
Legs and Feet—Black or slightly silvered on all four legs.	10
Eyes—Large and bold, color deep ruby.	10
Ears—Black, set apart, large and dropping.	10
Shape, Coat Condition and Color—To conform to the requirements of the self cavy, full of type and cobby throughout. Coat short and silky. To handle firm and be of good size.	20
	100

Remarks:
The white blaze is the desired head marking but otherwise good animals not to be unduly penalized for other head markings which present a well balanced appearance. A plain belly is not penalized, but the more spotting the better. Excessive roaning on body or belly is penalized. Type and shape to conform to the requirements of the Self Cavy; lack of type to be penalized. Black Dalmatian eye color is ruby, but when in shadow this may show as gray blue; also some Dalmatians with large eyes may have a blue-gray ring around the eye. This is not a fault. Colored Dalamatians must conform to the respective color requirements as set down by the English Self Cavy Club or in agoutis, the British National Agouti Cavy Club. The eye color must conform to the requirements as set down by the E.S.C.C. and B.N.A.C.C.
Fatty eye or side whiskers are disqualifications.

Although cavies are not born naked but fully coated, light-colored breeds are not easy to identify at birth. Dark-colored Selfs and marked varieties are readily recognizable.

All other things being equal, a well groomed cavy will have a slight edge over one that is not clean or neat.

CRESTEDS

The standard for the English Crested is:

Crest—matching body color	20
Color—conforms to colors of the matching British English Self	24
Shape—short, cobby, deep broad shoulder	20
Coat—short and silky	12
Ears—rose petal shaped, set wide apart, slightly drooping	8
Eyes—large and bold	8
Condition—	8
	100

Remarks:

The crest should radiate from a center point between the eyes and ears. The crest is a deep rosette, the lower edge is well down the nose. Any different colored hairs in the crest will be severely penalized. An abundance of different colored hairs on the body will be penalized.

Since this variety of Crested resembles the colors of the Self cavy, study the section on the Selfs for information. With regard to the crest, this radiates from the center pinpoint with hairs distributed evenly around.

Faults arise in the head, shape or type, coat, depth of color and colored hairs over the body. The crest is sometimes poorly formed and is placed too high on the head, seeming too small; the surrounding hair might stand erect and is not circled. Often the base is slanting instead of level.

The standard for the American Crested:

Crest—contrasting to body color	20
Color—body color conforms to colors of matching British "English Self"	24
Shape—short, cobby body, deep broad shoulders	20
Ears—rose petal shaped, set wide and slightly drooping	8
Coat—short and silky	12
Eyes—large and bold	8
Condition—	8
	100

Remarks:

The crest should be as near to a complete circle of solid color as possible. A circle of less than seventy-five per cent

Extreme pigmentation is represented in the Black Self and varying degrees of pigmentation in very light-colored selfs. Total absence of pigmentation in the eye results in pink eyes. Photo by Brian Seed.

will be severely penalized. The crest color should not appear elsewhere on the body. A blaze of crest color will be severely penalized. Hairs of body color in the crest will be penalized.

The American Cresteds are judged in exactly the same way as the British English Cresteds, except that the crest must have a different color from that of the body color. If the contrasting color of hairs in the crest is less than seventy-five per cent of the circle, it must be severely penalized. The color of the crest must not appear anywhere else on the body. If hairs the same color of the body appear in the crest, they must not be more than twenty-five per cent, and this contrasting color must not overlap beyond the circle of the crest onto the body.

According to American standards if the contrasting color of the crest is reduced by one-eigth or 12½% of the circle it is disqualified. Thus the body hairs should not overlap into the crest at the same extent.

Standard for the Himalayan Crested:
Crest—white to match body color	20
Color—conforms to colors of matching smooth Himalayans	24

Other points are the same as they are for the English Crested

The standard for the Agouti Crested:
Crest—matches body color	20
Color—matches color and pattern of corresponding smooth Agouti	24

Other points are the same as they are for the English Crested.

Crested varieties are also found in the Dutch, Tortoiseshell and White, Roan, Dalmatian and Sheltie. Unstandardized Cresteds must be in unstandardized classes but will be catered to at the Crested Cavy Club Stock Shows.

A banded variety of cavy. If the band is situated close to the head, a collar-like effect is created. Photo by M.F. Roberts.

RARE VARIETIES

The Tortoiseshell, Brindle, Bi-Color and Tri-Color have a Full Standard.

The Harlequins, Magpies, Black-Eyed Golden, Saffron and Argentes have a Guide Standard.

All other unstandardized varieties, including the Rex, are catered to by the British Rare Varieties Cavy Club.

Exhibiting Your Guinea Pig

Any novice fancier who wishes to exhibit his or her cavy should visit a show first to learn the principles of exhibiting.

Information on all of the breeds can be discussed with experienced fanciers when you visit your first show. You will be able to spend many happy hours at the show by meeting cavy breeders, chatting about cavies and forming friendships with other fanciers that can sometimes last a lifetime.

TABLE OR BOX SHOWS

In Great Britain you can attend two kinds of shows, one is a small afternoon show called a Table or Box Show and the other is a larger, all-day show called a Pen Show.

These shows are run by fanciers who belong to cavy or rabbit clubs. The clubs have a committee with members elected by ballot and upon payment of a yearly subscription fanciers are accepted as members and are given a Year Book. Your Year Book will contain the standards of all pure breeds which breeders aim for and judges judge on. There will also be rules that you must abide by. Once you are a member of a cavy club you will be eligible to compete for trophies or special prizes that may be offered by the various clubs.

If you, as a fancier, do not have friends acquainted with exhibiting, then the periodical on small livestock (previously referred to) will be helpful to you since it will contain the details about any cavy shows that are coming up. You must contact the secretary and ask for a schedule. The schedule

A trio of Dutch cavies with their numerous awards: ribbons, plaques and cups. Awards have very little monetary value, but winning an award reflects the contribution of a fancier or breeder to the hobby and the esteem of fellow club members. Photo by B. Seed.

is a booklet that gives the classification of various breeds, states if the show will be a Table (or Box) or a Pen Show, gives the name of the show's judge and will give the closing date for the accepted entries.

You can also go to your local pet shop and ask who their suppliers are. Chances are their cavies come from an experienced breeder who will be able to give you information pertaining to exhibiting cavies and who to get in touch with for up-coming shows.

4-H Clubs may have different standards and rules for exhibiting cavies but a younger individual can start with such a club and join a more specialized cavy club later. For your first exhibition you should really take your cavy to a Table Show. It will be a training center for both you and your pet. You will learn the procedure for showing and your cavy will become acquainted with strange noises, large numbers of people and handling at the judging table.

When you first glance at the schedule you may become a bit confused when you see all of the abbreviated words. It is very important that you understand these abbreviations. They may appear as follows:

A.C.	Any Color
A.O.C.	Any Other Color
A.V.	Any Variety
A.O.V.	Any Other Variety
A.A.	Any Age
B or S	Boar or Sow
Ad.	Adult
D.	Duplicate
Breeders	Breeders of the Cavy
u/5 mos.	Under five months
Intermediate 5/8 mos.	Over five months but under eight months

Abbreviations used in cavy shows in the United States include the following:

B.I.S.	Best in Show
B.O.B.	Best of Breed
B.O.S.	Best of Opposite Sex
B.O.V.	Best of Variety
A.O.V.	Any Other Variety
B or S	Boar or Sow
Sr.	Senior—any boar or sow over six months or 30 ounces
Int.	Intermediate—any boar or sow from four to six months old and over 22 ounces and under and including 30 ounces.
Jr.	Junior—any boar or sow up to four months of age with a maximum weight of 22 ounces

There will also be reference made to the Junior fancier's classes or Youth fancier's classes in the U.S. The age limit for these young people is usually from seven to sixteen years. The Juniors can exhibit either pure breeds in their specified classes or cross-breeds which include pure breeds that have faults to the Standard of Merit and are not suitable for their own classes.

If you are not able to attend a show prior to your first exhibition, here is an example of the classes shown in British cavy clubs:

1. Self Black Ad.
2. Self A.C. u/5 mos.
3. Self A.O.C. ad.
4. Abyssinian T & W ad. (Tortoiseshell and White)
5. Abyssinian A.O.C. ad.
6. Dutch A.A. etc., etc.
19. A.O.V. u/5 mos.
20. A.O.V. ad.
21. Self Breeders ad.
22. Non-Self Breeders ad.
23. Non-Self Breeders u/5 mos.
24. Self Breeders u/5 mos.
25. Challenge Sow A.A.
26. Challenge Boar A.A.
27. Grand Challenge A.V. A.A.

Some of the cavy breeds exhibited in the United States are the American, Abbysinian, Peruvian, American Crested, Silky and other new breeds. Depending on the rules of a club, new introductions may be accepted under certain limitations or provisional conditions. Each of these breeds is also grouped into Selfs, Solids, Agoutis and Marked. They are generally entered in show room classes limited by sex, weight and age: Junior, Intermediate and Senior Boars and Sows.

ENTRY FORM

The first space on a typical British entry form is for the pen number of the cavy, issued by the secretary. The second space is the breed class. The third space is for use by duplicate classes. The fourth space is the cavy's description. The fifth space is the entry fee.

Suppose that you want to exhibit a Self White sow under five months. Look to see if there is a class of its own color, as it must go into its breed class first. As there is not a class for Self White, it must go into class number two which covers Any Color Self under five months. The cavy had been bred by you, so it can also be entered into class twenty-four; if you do not feel that it is an outstanding exhibit, there is no need to duplicate it into any more classes. Suppose that you also want to exhibit a Roan Abyssinian adult boar, bred by you. Again, there is no class for its color, so you must enter him into class five, and if you wish you can duplicate it into classes twenty-two, twenty-six and twenty-seven. A Red Dutch sow of only fair markings need not be duplicated at all; it will just go into its breed class six.

Should you find that a separate class for your cavy is not available, you must keep it as a Self with its breed in the A.O.C. In the case of the Agouti, Himalayan and Peruvian, if there is not a breed class they must be entered in the A.O.V. of the Non-Self section.

When you have filled in the entry form, send it in to the secretary with the proper fees before the closing date. In return you will receive ear labels with pen numbers at the show for each one of your cavies. (Ear labels will be discussed later.) Some small Table Shows accept entries up to one hour before the judging begins.

At your first show do not enter your cavy into every duplicate class that is applicable. As a new fancier, you may think that you have an outstanding cavy and will not notice some of the faults that a judge will. It would be very disappointing for you to have your cavy placed very low in its

Award _____ No. in class _____ Special _____

Head _____ Ears _____ Bone _____

Type _____ Wt. _____ Cond. _____

Color _____ Fur _____

Remarks _____

_____

_____

_____ Judge _____

Breed _____ Date _____ X

Class _____ Sex _____ Ear No. _____ X

Exhibitor _____ X

Show _____ X

. . . .

Exhibitor No.   Rabbit No.

_____

For Secretary's
Use Only ►_____

Breed _____ X

Class _____ Sex _____ Ear No. _____ X

Award _____ No. in class _____ Judge _____

Exhibitor _____ X

Address _____ X

City _____ State _____ X

Local Club _____ X

Exhibitor please fill in blanks marked 'X'

class after you had been thinking that it was so outstanding. If it were to be placed very low in the class, it would not be awarded a prize in the duplicate classes where all breeds meet, because entries from other classes would be placed over it after they had won prizes in their own classes. You must learn by experience. If your cavy gets on quite well in its first show, then the duplicating can be extended at the next show. You must remember that judges' opinions differ with exhibits; one judge may put a cavy down in the awards and the next judge may place it quite high.

In the United States a cavy can be entered into only one class at a show. If you wanted to enter an American White sow that is between four and six months old and over 22 ounces and under 30 ounces, you would fill out the card as follows:

Judge:	John Doe
Breed:	American White
Date:	1/25/79
Class:	Intermediate
Exhibitor:	S. Hutt
Show:	Big City
Ear No.:	H1

EAR LABELS

What happens at a Table-Box Show in Great Britain? Having previously sent your entry form to the secretary, go to the person who is distributing ear labels at the show when you arrive. Give your name if you are not known and you will be given an envelope containing the labels with the

An example of an entry form with a tear-off section. This permits the secretary and stewards to locate cavies participating in a show.

A cavy in a holding pen with the ear label in position. Photo by E. Jukes.

pen numbers written on them. Ask for a piece of chalk. Check that the numbers correspond correctly with the classes in which you have entered your cavy. If more than one cavy is entered, the breed and the duplicate class numbers will be stated on the face of the envelope. Stick the small ear labels securely on the cavy's ear and mark the same number on the top of the outside compartment of the carrying case in chalk. Place the box in numerical order on the floor with the other fanciers' boxes.

In the United States the left ear is tagged (either with a permanent metal tag or with a piece of tape) with numbers and/or letters corresponding with those on the entry blank.

170

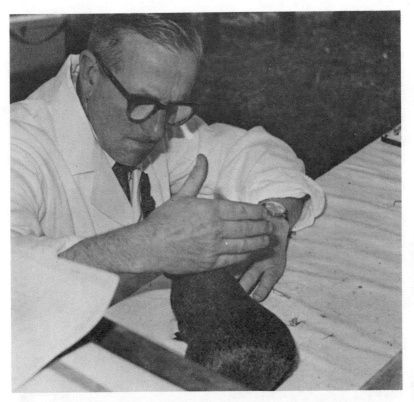

A judge engrossed in his job during a show in England. For protection against the sun, and possibly rain, the show is often held under a big tent. Photo by E. Jukes.

JUDGING TABLE AND BOOK

The judging table is exactly the same whether the show is a Pen Show or a Table Show, or a one-day show or a National Convention in the United States. Judging tables are set up and covered with sheeting or burlap. A small stool or box is used for sitting the cavy on for assessing all-around quality before close examination. This box is placed close to the judging pens that are on the judging table. Judging pens were introduced to the cavy fancy by my husband, R. T. R. Elward about twenty-five years ago, these pens are like open-topped boxes joined together, usually six inches high, seven inches wide, and have a low front of

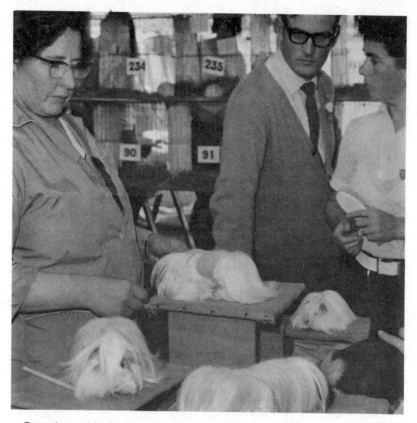

Peruvians sitting on burlap-covered platforms for judging. Note that the steward or owner has a brush ready, if needed. Photo by E. Jukes.

three inches. One box accommodates one cavy while the class is being judged. The judging pens were given the name of "Honest Steward," meaning never leaving the judge.

It is the practice of some stewards or carriers, as they are called in the United States, to help until their classes are judged, then they disappear. It is poor stewarding when a judge has to call for a steward or carrier while he is in the middle of judging.

It is the duty of the stewards or carrier to look after the cavies on the table and to see that they are never unattended, especially when they are being returned to their boxes or to their pens. They also keep a watch on the ear labels and make sure that they do not come off as the cavy is brought to the table. They make certain that the cavies that are in the pens are put on the table in the numerical order that corresponds with the judging book.

As the cavies are placed on the judging table, their sex is noted in the judging book by the judge against the pen number—this is a great help in cases where an ear label falls off and the cavies are all the same color. Just by noting the sex, the mix-up can be straightened out.

The judging book has a page made out for each class and will contain the pen numbers of each cavy entered in the appropriate classes. All of the judging is done by the numbers that the cavy wears on the ears. As the judge examines each cavy, notes are made in the judging book regarding the merit of the cavy. After completion of a class, the judge signs the judging slip that tears from the book. Once he has signed this slip, the awards are final and cannot be altered. This slip is then given to the secretary who then enters the awards against the names entered in the class and the prizes are given out. At Table Shows these prizes are left for fanciers to collect at the end of the show with the prize money, but at Pen Shows the prize cards are displayed on the pens and the prize money is either collected or mailed to fanciers.

In America the judge's remarks are recorded slightly differently. You fill out a comment card that you give to the secretary prior to the judging. It will be used in identifying the animal by matching the numbers with those found on the cavy's ear. As the judge examines each cavy, comments regarding the merits of the cavy are noted on the card. After the completion of the show, awards are given out at the show or mailed out. The second half of the comment card is also available after judging; on this you will be able to find what place you received and how many were in your class.

PEN SHOWS

The only difference between Table Shows and Pen Shows is that in Pen Shows, wire mesh pens of about twelve square inches are used. These pens are bedded with sawdust or hay. The cavies remain in their pens during the hours of the show. Judging usually starts at about 10:30 in the morning; there are two or more judges. The cavy's ear labels correspond with those of the labels on the pens. When the labels have been put on the cavies, the fanciers then put their cavies into their appropriate pens.

Some Pen Shows do not have judging pens for the table; instead the carrying boxes are placed end to end along the judging table, forming a platform with a smaller box at each end and one in the middle. Sows are placed in one side, boars in the other. As they are judged they are placed along the table, forming a platform and attended by the stewards.

For obvious reasons the judging is held at a distance from the spectators.

Rear view of holding pens.

In pen shows in the U.S. the cavies may stay from one night to one week depending on the show. During these shows the animals may be kept in coops or in carrying cases. If they are placed in coops, these are usually marked with a specified number which tells the secretary what breed and variety is in the coop. The carriers can go directly to the coop and bring that cavy to the judging table.

RAIL TRANSPORT

At very large shows in Great Britain cavies are accepted by rail, but it is a very expensive way of exhibiting them. To exhibit by rail you would send your entry in the usual way to the secretary and you would receive rail labels in return. These have the show's address on them and under the tear-off flap, your name and address would be inserted for the return journey. The round-trip fare must be paid for at the time you send your exhibit. Exhibition boxes are required when cavies are sent by railway.

Mark clearly on the rail label where it gives pen number (ear label) your cavy's breed and age; also put this information on a slip of paper inside the box, above the cavy. This avoids any mistakes if more than one color of the same breed is sent and all are not duplicated. A steward would not know this unless you gave proper instructions. All cavies that are sent to shows are attended by the stewards at the show; they are fed and cared for at the show and are given food for the trip home.

SHOW ETHICS

While you watch the judging at a show, it is quite all right to steward or to stand by while the judging is taking place, but do not discuss your cavies at the table with another fancier within hearing of the judge. It will not matter to the judge that you are talking about a particular cavy because he judges by the ear label; it is, however, rather disturbing when a general conversation is being held while the judge is trying to assess a cavy.

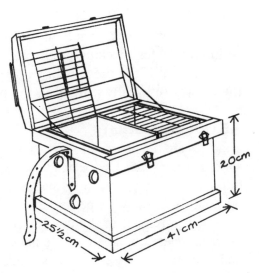

Diagrammatic illustration of a traveling case suited for cavies. Peruvians, in particular, require careful handling during transport.

JUDGING PROBLEMS

When there are two or more judges, they jointly judge various duplicate classes and then the examining is reversed. What one judge has already judged, the other examines and makes a final decision on the cavy that will take the awards of the duplicate classes. Sometimes it happens that the two judges cannot agree, each preferring his own choice. When this happens, a referee judge who has not exhibited at the show is called in to make a final choice of cavies. When the referee judge has made a decision, it is final and cannot be altered.

At times confusion does arise about an exhibit being the Best in Show. Some fanciers think that a cavy that wins the Challenge classes is the outright winner. This is not so; it is only the winner of named duplicate class. Any cavy that has won its breed class, has not been duplicated to any other class, or is of better merit than that of the winner of the challenges can be declared that Best in Show. Best in Show means that the cavy excels on all points of the Standard of the specified breed.

After a judge has completed judging, you may ask his or her opinion of the stock that was judged. It is best to take your prize cards with you; then it is much easier to see the pen numbers for checking up the notes about the cavy that is concerned. If the judge is in a hurry to leave, reports of the shows are usually printed in the periodicals.

AFTER THE SHOW

Cavies are not allowed to be taken away from the show as soon as their class has been judged if they are not in the duplicating classes. No cavy may be removed from a show without the secretary's permission. At Pen Shows they are expected to remain in the pens or coops until judging has been completed, unless fanciers have very long trips ahead and have been excused by the secretary.

If you have taken several boxes and cavies to the show, make a final check before you leave to be certain that you are taking all of your stock home with you. Many times fanciers get all the way home and find that they have left a cavy or two at the show. This causes quite a lot of inconvenience for the secretary, who either has to house the cavy or has to find another fancier who can house it until the cavy is retrieved.

Hints on Grooming and Preparation of Your Cavy

When you first visited a cavy show you may have noticed the types of cavies that received awards. A number of smooth-coated cavies were well presented, meaning that the coat had been groomed or beautified, resulting in sleek appearance. Had they not been groomed the coats would have appeared dull with hairs of uneven length over the top of the body.

Grooming and washing of the cavy, details of which will be explained in this chapter, are all that are allowed by the British cavy clubs and American cavy clubs. "An exhibit has to be disqualified if in the opinion of the judges it has been subjected to practices calculated to deceive or to give false impression of merit." They must be exhibited in a perfectly natural condition.

When you are breeding cavies for exhibition, you look for exhibition potential shortly after birth. From an early age, you handle your cavy frequently to train it for the quietness he will need to display at the shows. It has to learn to sit still on the judging table, not being held by the judge's stewards. It will be unable to show off its fine qualities if it is frightened and tries to run off the table.

A cavy of any variety must have a quiet disposition. It will stand little chance of winning if the judge is unable to sit it on a stool or a box lid on the judging table to assess its general qualities. This is required for any pure breed that is judged to standard rules.

The author, holding a cavy.

To train your cavy to sit on a stool or a box lid you should not begin the task at a distance too high from the ground. A chair (with a piece of burlap on the seat for the cavy to dig its toe nails into) is a good training height; if your cavy falls from the chair, it is not so likely to get hurt from this height. You must take special care until the time that it can sit contentedly on the chair unattended. It is during training that a fall can cause a cavy's teeth to become broken. Gradually raise the height of the training level to a table of about four and one-half feet, the equivalent of the judging table.

A cavy can also be trained to sit still by alternately petting it and setting it on a counter or table everyday so it can get used to the idea of sitting while not being petted.

GROOMING SMOOTH-COATED VARIETIES

During the training to sit still you can begin to groom your cavy. You do this in smooth-coated varieties by first stroking it from head to rump with both hands. After stroking, make long sweeps down the body with the sides of your thumb, preferably dampened. These sweeps are for taking out long guard hairs that protect the finer undercoat; if swept in this manner the hair will not be patchy or uneven.

For the novice fancier the art of grooming needs a lot of practice. It is best that you practice on a cavy that is not needed for exhibition so that the right pressure of the thumbs can be learned. At first it can be just another setback, as too much or too little grooming can make a cavy lose position or awards.

If your cavy is to be exhibited in an upcoming show, you should start to groom it about three weeks before the show. Excessive grooming in a short period of time causes a cavy to lose condition rapidly. Extended over three weeks or so, the cavy would then not be back in firm condition.

When you are grooming, you must apply firm pressure by your thumb, otherwise the guard hairs will not come

Peruvians (Shelties also) while waiting in the pens at a show can get their hair entangled with the hay that may be present. Since a judge is allowed to straighten stray hairs, a brush should be handy during the judging. Photo by C. Eurich.

out. At this stage your cavy's coat will look dull, dusty and thick because of the presence of dead hairs. These dead hairs are easily removed with a few sweeps of the thumb. You must also groom the sides or flank; do not forget the face because the hairs on the face often look rather coarse. Make a few sweeps up from the nose through the forehead and cheeks and then go down the back. You must release some of the pressure in the center as the hair in this part is always very thin. When over-groomed, this can produce an uneven appearance or bare patches in the skin; it will take about six weeks for the hair to grow back to full length. Be very careful when you go over the hip bones because you can easily catch your thumb here, causing bare patches over the rump. Sit your cavy so that nothing will interrupt the long sweeps that you will be making.

Go over the hair sweeping it between your thumb and your first finger. If guard hairs still protrude, use a suede shoe brush, going crosswise for final touches in removing uneven hairs.

You should then hold your cavy on your hand and check for uneven side hairs and lower rump hairs that were hidden from you while your cavy was sitting on the chair. Go around these areas with your damp thumb and your first finger to groom them evenly.

Grooming is not an easy matter to learn from written instructions; it would be easier for you to watch an experienced fancier who could better explain the proper method. You would then see the correct way and amount of pressure to be used.

You will notice that your hands will get very dirty while you groom your cavy. This is just a combination of dust collected from such things as sawdust, shavings, hay and grease from the cavy's hair.

Once your cavy has gained enough confidence to sit unattended on the chair, the next thing to do is to make a small wire mesh pen (one foot square) equivalent to a show pen. Put your cavy into this pen for a few hours each day. Feed him in the pen so that he becomes accustomed to being in the pen. When the time comes take your cavy to a show and it is placed in a similar pen, it will not be frightened. As previously mentioned, anything strange to a cavy will likely frighten it.

Being shut in an exhibition box or carrying case can distress your cavy. If this occurs, when you arrive at the show it will be huddled in the corner of the box and will feel limp when you handle it. An exhibition cavy must be in firm condition so it is best that you train it to overcome its fear of being enclosed. Place it in the carrying case for about an hour for the first day and then extend the time. When it has lost its fear of the case, give it some food so that it learns to eat in it for future trips to cavy shows.

The final preparation comes just one week before the show. Your cavy will need a bath to cleanse the hair and skin and to remove lice, nits and dirt from the coat. The lice are very small but they irritate the skin. When badly infested, the lice can be seen moving in the hair and in this condition—quite often some cavies are exhibited in this state—they pass the lice to other cavies on the judging table. There is also another type of lice that appears like fine dust over the hair. The lice are passed from one cavy to another or come along with poor quality hay. However, they do not live on human beings, cats, or dogs.

Washing your cavy will take very little time. Some cavies are distressed on the first wetting but after several minutes are not upset by being in the water. You will need a plastic bowl with a piece of toweling in the bottom to prevent your cavy from slipping. Medicated shampoos should be used as they rid cavies of lice and will kill off the sarcoptic mite that has been prevalent during the past four years. This mite burrows under the skin of a cavy, causing great distress.

Put about two inches of warm water in the bowl and thoroughly wet your cavy's hair. Apply the shampoo, working up a lather that spreads over the body. Wash the inside of the ears too, because mites congregate in them. Leave the shampoo on it for at least five minutes; if you wish, you can wrap it in a towel to keep it from shaking the shampoo off. Put your cavy back into the shampoo water; gently scrub the feet, between the toes, and the toenails with a nail brush. With adult boars, the "grease spot" at the tail stump section will need attention. This spot gets very dirty; if you miss it when you give him a bath, he may lose points when being judged. It is best to apply a kitchen washing liquid on the spot with your finger tip; let it soak into the grease for a few minutes, then use the nail brush and the shampoo water and the spot should come clean.

Look behind the ears to see if there are nits (louse eggs) attached to the hairs; they are white in color. The nits will

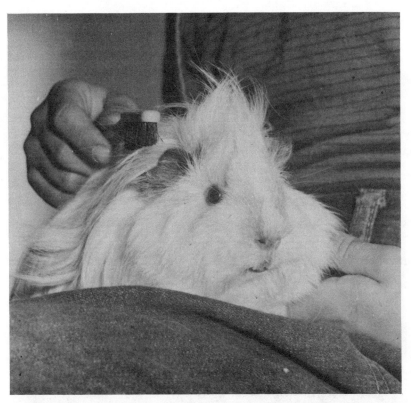

An ordinary toothbrush is useful in removing grime, dirt and nits (if present) from individual hairs. Photo by M. F. Roberts.

not come off during the washing but by using a toothbrush and brushing the hair against the way it is growing, the nits will slide off the hairs.

You can now rinse your cavy in warm water and towel it dry. You can use a blow-dryer or put it in a box and keep it warm in the house until the hair dries. In the winter do not return your cavy to an outside hutch until the following day. This prevents nighttime chilling after being freshly washed. This risk can also be avoided by not keeping cavies in an outside hutch during winter.

Once the hair has settled down after washing and its natural sheen has returned, continue grooming the coat by using a piece of silk cloth and a soft-bristled brush.

185

Cavies are housed singly in show pens. Damage from fighting is thus avoided. Hay will keep them warm and contented. Stewards, of course, give them food and water during their stay. Photo by C. Eurich.

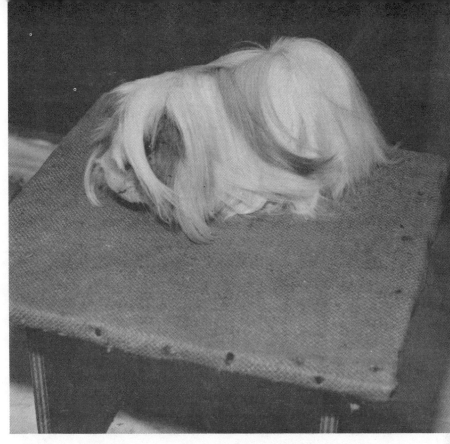

Platforms or stools for showing long-haired varieties can also be used for grooming in the home. Photo by E. Jukes.

Abyssinians will need their ears, feet and stomach cleaned prior to exhibiting. The harsh hair and the rosettes can be brushed with a stiff-bristled brush; the rosettes should be attended to singly. The crested variety needs the same body grooming as a smooth-coated variety; the crest on the forehead should be brushed with a tooth brush.

Always leave sufficient time before leaving for a show to check your cavy's mouth, feet, and stomach for overnight stains, and re-check on arrival at the show. Grooming and washing are not judged as giving a false impression of merit. In a variety with a thick coat these steps have to be carried out, because of the possible presence of lice, grease, and dead hair.

It is not until a sleek coat has been obtained that a true top and undercolor are assured. It is a well-known adage that "the shorter the coat, the better the color." Long coats show flakiness, meaning a lighter undercolor is seen because long hair does not carry its color to the full extent of each hair.

Whatever the breed is that you exhibit, your aim is to win an award and to have your exhibit look its best. Your exhibit should not be ungroomed, dirty, in poor condition, have skin blemishes or carry lice.

GROOMING LONG-HAIRED VARIETIES

The grooming and conditioning of the Peruvian is totally different from the method used for the smooth varieties.

When your Peruvian is a few weeks old, you can begin to train him to be quiet and to get accustomed to being groomed.

When you groom your Peruvians, use a brush or a comb and you must have a separate brush or comb for each one of your Peruvians. If the scent from one cavy is passed on to another it could result in one of them biting pieces out of its own hair to rid itself of the other's scent.

The hair, which will eventually be very long, grows at the rate of roughly one inch per month. With care the hair can be kept in a showable condition for about eighteen months to two years. Naturally the cavy cannot trail this very long hair around in its hutch, so you must put it in wrappers (described later in this chapter).

Any long-haired variety should be kept on sawdust or wood shavings (some American fanciers use rice hulls) because the hair could get damaged on a bedding of hay; the hay for eating should be kept in a tied-up bundle in the hutch or bought in special cube form (available in the U.S.). If you feel that a hay bedding is necessary, then the hay should be cut up into short lengths to stop your cavy from burrowing under it. By burrowing, the cavy would be

To avoid damage to the coat of long-haired breeds, loose hay should not be placed in the pen during a show. Other materials, like sawdust or rice hulls, are more appropriate. Photo by C. Eurich.

spoiled for exhibition because the hair of the frontal or fringe and on the sides of the shoulders would become dragged out.

When your Peruvian is about eight weeks old and is used to being brushed and is quiet, the rear sweep (the hair from the hindquarters) will then be a few inches long and will start to become urine-stained. This could spoil the hair. To prevent this damage, put the hair into a wrapper. Most fanciers place, in adults, a wrapper on each side, one on the rear sweep. These should not allow the hair to curl at the ends. The wrappers look like neat little parcels; once the hair is long they are undone only for the cavy to be brushed or for presentation on the judging table.

The first time that you place a wrapper on your young cavy, it may scratch or bite it off, especially if it is rather tight and the hairs are being pulled. Always make sure that the wrapper is comfortable. If your cavy removes it, keep trying until it gets used to it. Some never get used to the wrapper and are not suitable for exhibition. If this is the case, use them for breeding stock and keep their hair clipped back.

To make a wrapper you will need a piece of brown paper (some people use cotton cloth instead) that is three inches wide and four inches long. Fold it into three sections length-wise with one end turned over one-half inch to make a fold. In the center section place a piece of balsa wood, three-quarters of an inch wide, under the folded end and seal the whole fold across so that the wood cannot slip out. (Some exhibitors do not use balsa wood at all.) Fold the sides into the middle so that the wrapper looks like a flat oblong and then fold it lengthwise to make accordion pleats that are about one inch apart. The wrapper is now ready. As your cavy grows and the length of its hair increases, you will need to increase the size of the wrapper too.

Study the photographs of the Peruvian having its hair put into a wrapper. Place your cavy on a box or a stool and make one part down the center of the back and another across the rump. The parting should resemble the letter "T." The head of the T takes the hair from the sweep; this is the only section that will need to be wrapped for a young cavy. When your cavy is four to five months old it will also need to have a wrapper on each of the sides. The stroke of the letter T is the dividing line down the middle of the back. It takes the hair from the sides and includes the frontal, which is brushed to each side. The hair from the parting is then brushed down to the lower sides and is ready for wrapping.

Take the wrapper in one hand and the hair from the sweep in the other. Place the hair in the center fold of the wrapper; make sure that the end of the wrapper that has no balsa wood in it is against your cavy's body. Turn the sides in and fold up the wrapper in accordion folds so that the end of the wrapper faces downwards, preventing sawdust and dirt from getting into it and damaging the hair. Secure the balsa wood and wrapper with an elastic band; it will appear to be a small parcel. This method is good for any Peruvian once its hair is long enough to wrap.

To wash your Peruvian you will need a bowl of warm water, three or four inches deep. Place a piece of toweling in the bottom of the bowl to prevent your cavy from slipping. Have the medicated shampoo, warm rinsing water and dry towels at hand.

Unwrap your cavy's hair and brush it out. Place the cavy in the water and hold it with one hand at all times; if it should panic, it could get the back feet and toenails tangled in the wet hair and cause damage.

Never rub the shampoo in the hair for this will cause the hair to tangle. You should gently squeeze the coat after shampooing. Rinse your cavy several times with the warm water, then lift it out of the bowl and let the water drain off. Place it on a dry towel or on any absorbent material and pat the hair to remove the moisture.

Do not rub the hair with the towel because the tangling that results could damage the hair for exhibition. It is best to dry the hair with a blow-dryer. Once you have completely dried the hair you can brush it and put it back in the wrappers. Like any other cavy that has recently been washed, do not put it in an outside hutch immediately, but wait until the next day.

The habits of the Peruvian and the Sheltie (Silky) are very similar. One important thing for you to remember is

191

that the young ones that show exhibition potential should be housed on their own soon after weaning because they often chew or nibble on each other's hair. Such damage to their hair would leave them suitable only for breeding stock.

Once either of these varieties are on the judging table, it is against the rules to brush their hair. You should, however, bring your cavy's brush to the judging table because the judge is allowed to brush the hair if it has been disarranged during the examination. Once the judging has commenced, either of the long-haired varieties are allowed to be brushed for presentation only. No other form of grooming may be used.

For grooming a Sheltie, carry out the instructions given for the Peruvian. The instructions differ somewhat only in the wrapping and in the brushing. The Sheltie's hair is brushed from the mane or head furnishing to the rear sweep, as it does not have a center parting. Usually only one wrapper is required and it is placed on the sweep. If fanciers wish, they also have wrappers on the sides.

The procedure for washing the Sheltie is the same as it is for the Peruvian.

Complaints, Illnesses, and Diseases

Cavies or guinea pigs, whether kept as pets or for exhibition are generally very healthy. Like any species, however, they can contract a number of diseases. In the course of this chapter a large number of diseases will be discussed. These are given as a guide in case your cavy becomes ill.

You must remember that quality and not quantity is required when breeding exhibition stock. A small selected breeding stock is all that you need to produce prize-winners. As previously mentioned, it is a mistake to think that you need a large stud to breed cavies that are suitable for exhibition. It is through excessive breeding that the number of cavies in your stud will grow out of hand and beyond your financial limits. When your stud grows beyond your control, you will have too many cavies being housed together. They will be poorly fed and will not have sufficient hay to act as a reserve food. Serious outbreaks of diseases will occur in a badly managed stud that is kept undernourished and under poor hygienic conditions.

Your cavy's most common complaint will be a slight stomach upset which usually occurs as the result of a feeding error. In severe weather it may catch a cold and you will hear coughing and wheezing. Both of these are curable and will be discussed later.

SIGNS OF ILLNESS

To prevent serious diseases from spreading, it is important that you know what effect they will have on your cavy and what it will look like when it is ill.

Usually the first sign that a cavy is ill will be that it will not eat. You will see that it is huddled and hunch-backed, has very dull eyes and the hair will be standing out all over its body, giving it a spikey appearance known as "open coat." It will be limp when you handle it. It may also have acute diarrhea. If the cavy is in this state, it is very ill and must be isolated. Some fanciers prefer to take the healthy cavies from the infected hutch and leave the ill ones there. Others prefer to destroy those that are sick to prevent further outbreaks.

The really distressing thing about sick cavies is that once they have stopped eating, they usually put their heads into the corner of the hutch and have no will to fight disease or to live; they can be dead within hours. It is because of the cavy's lack of cooperation and its complete submission to disease that many fanciers put their sick cavies out of their misery. Cavies that recover from contagious diseases usually become carriers and outbreaks will occur when they are returned to the stud.

Whether it is a growing cavy or an adult, if it has a serious illness and will not eat, it will lose considerable condition. It seldom regains perfect health or remains in firm condition for any length of time. Sickness stunts the growth of cavies that are a few months old.

You will often find that sick cavies can suffer from several diseases at the same time. This bears out the theory that even though it is very hard to part with any cavy, the very ill ones should be destroyed, because any illness leaves permanent damage. Should you have to destroy any of your cavies, do so in the quickest possible way. Never submit them to drowning; it is a very cruel way to destroy them.

HUTCH HYGIENE

The shed should always have a flow of fresh air through it no matter how cold the weather may be. Air vents have been previously mentioned. It is better to house cavies in a

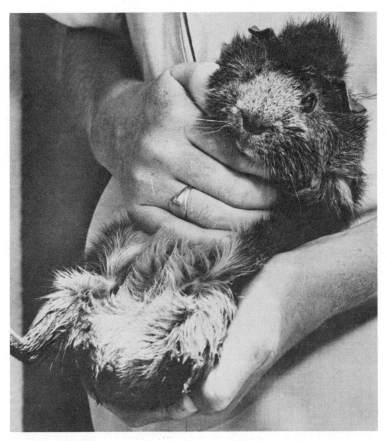

The cause of wet vent in cavies should always be investigated. It can be a sign of serious intestinal or urinary ailments. Photo by L. van der Meid.

cool shed with plenty of ventilation and bedding for warmth than to have a heated shed with closed ventilators. With this latter type of shed, there will be stale air throughout the shed, along with high humidity. Condensation will be running down the windows and dripping from the inside of the roof. Electric fans are used to reduce the humidity, because often with high humidity outbreaks of lung complaints and diarrhea are more common.

It must be remembered that drafts kill cavies, not the winter weather. If the temperature does drop exceedingly

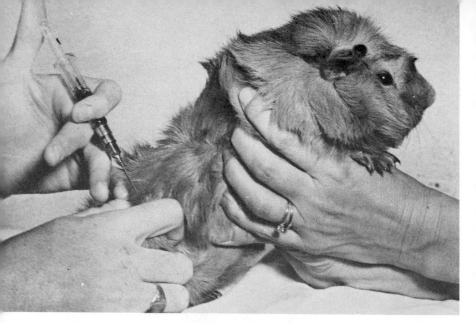

There are some cavy diseases that are controlled by the proper inoculation. The procedure should be undertaken only with the advice of a veterinarian. Photo by L. van der Meid.

low take special care to provide warmth for them. This should include feeding to create body heat and energy because when a cavy becomes chilled and cold it becomes languid and illness sets in. With any form of illness, body heat is essential.

Most diseases have an acute and chronic form and there are a number of ways in which cavies contract them. Some diseases lie dormant in a cavy's body, developing later in times of stress or with poor housing and feeding management.

To achieve and maintain good health in your cavies keep clean hutches and disinfect the shed, feeding dishes and water drinkers. Hutches that badly need cleaning and have too many cavies housed together are the breeding grounds for disease.

Rats, mice, and flies are the main carriers of contagious diseases. At the first trace of vermin an exterminator should be called in. The droppings from rats and mice that contaminate cavies' food and hay can cause such contagious diseases that a whole stud may die. Even a few stray mice can cause a major outbreak. Always keep food covered to prevent contamination.

If you train a kitten to live in the cavy shed, it can kill off any mice. The kitten will not attack or disturb young or adult cavies if it is brought up with them. It is the stray marauding cats and their fierce fights that cause terror to cavies. The fierce fighting of cats, barking dogs and loud noises such as those caused by a carpenter at work are very disturbing to in-pig sows and can cause miscarriages and abortions. The cavies will become accustomed to everyday noises but not to noises or high-pitched tones which can cause panic in a shed, usually followed by illness of in-pig sows.

Flies must be exterminated quickly; they spread disease by fouling the food and entering the hutches. There are

Guinea pigs should on occasion be allowed some freedom out-doors. Sunshine is beneficial, unless the exposure is so long that the cavies get overheated. Photo by B. Seed.

various ways of killing off flies. Some fanciers use fly-killing strips or sprays. Using these is controversial. Some fanciers feel the vapors are harmful to cavies, the hay and the feed. Other breeders feel they cause the stock to be sterile. Therefore, you must use your own judgment and use whatever you have confidence in. Fly paper is still procurable and is very satisfactory for keeping sheds free of flies.

Bird droppings on green food can cause outbreaks of disease, so should the food become soiled, wash it and allow it to dry before feeding it to your cavies. Chemical sprays may have been used on vegetable greens, so it is best to wash them if you are unsure about how they were grown.

Many fanciers treat their own cavies for minor diseases and this is one of the many points discussed when fanciers meet at shows. Early diagnosis can lead to successful treatment and cure.

Recognizing various symptoms of illness is vital to anyone who has cavies, because contagious diseases will spread quickly through persons who handle an infected animal.

Cavies have been used for medical research for a great many years, but not enough has been learned about them yet to treat their various illnesses. They are such small animals that there is difficulty in administering the correct dosage.

If cavies begin to die during an outbreak of a serious disease, consult a veterinarian. A postmortem examination may be necessary in order to identify the disease of the dead cavies.

ANTIBIOTICS

Antibiotics are widely used for illnesses but should not be administered without full knowledge of their use. Some of the ones that can be used are Tetracycline for lung complaints and Chloramphenicol for stomach upsets such as diarrhea. Penicillin should not be used for any diseases. It is best to consult your veterinarian for the appropriate medication and dosage.

Antibiotics should never be used as a precaution. Do not give it by mouth to cavies, for it can cause harm by upsetting the stomach. Often it is the treatment and not the disease that kills cavies.

ISOLATION

To isolate a sick cavy from your healthy ones, just house it away from them. It is essential that the healthy cavies are fed before you feed and attend to your sick one. After attending to your sick cavy, always scrub your finger nails since germs are very easily carried under them. You should use a disinfected mat when going from one shed to another.

Cavies in isolation need a lot of attention. They should be offered small amounts of dry mixed cereals, together with hay. If the cavy does not have diarrhea, you can give it small amounts of green food. If it does have diarrhea, from a stomach upset, it will show as loose droppings. Offer him raspberry or bramble leaves (with the thorns removed) or anything that is of an astringent nature. Any soiled food and bedding must be removed and be replaced by fresh food and bedding.

A sick cavy will have a very small appetite. Dehydration soon sets in when a cavy is ill. You must keep water available. If your cavy is not well enough to drink by itself, place the spout of the water bottle into its mouth and it may drink a little. Always sterilize the drinking spout and let your sick cavies have their own utensils. You must wash these utensils quite frequently.

If your cavy does not show any sign of improvement and you believe that it is suffering from a contagious disease, it would be best to destroy it.

Usually, fanciers who have lost a number of cavies during an outbreak of a contagious disease burn the dead bodies of the infected cavies. They also burn the bedding and some even burn the hutches. If the hutches are kept, they must be scrubbed out with a strong solution of household disinfectant in hot water. The hutches must remain empty for three weeks and disinfected again before using.

Whenever you purchase new stock, even if it has come from a reliable breeder, isolate it for at least two or three weeks.

Cavies that have come back from shows should have their feet washed and their bodies sprayed with pesticides (special prescriptions are available only from a veterinarian) in case they have come into contact with cavies that were carrying lice and mites. If you saw any loose droppings on the judging table at the show, isolate all the cavies that were at the show for several days to check for a serious outbreak of disease.

COPROPHAGY

This section does not refer to illnesses, but it should be included in this chapter because the subject causes a lot of worry to parents whose children have cavies. When the pet cavy eats its own droppings, the parents think that the guinea pig is either ill or has dirty habits. Many parents destroy the cavies thinking that the cavies would pass disease on to their children.

Coprophagy, or eating of its own droppings, is normal for a cavy. It is similar to a cow chewing its cud. The droppings that the cavy eats are not the dry ones that are on the bottom of the hutch. The cavy takes the droppings directly from its anus. If you were to look inside the cavy's mouth, you would see that the droppings are small and moist; their protein content is essential for keeping a cavy in health. When people buy cavies for pets they should be told about this behavior to save the animal from being destroyed. They should also be told about a problem, related to coprophagy, with some boars.

When a boar is a few years old, a hard lump may be felt inside the anus when handled. The boar will cry when the

200

lump is touched. What has happened is that the muscles of the bowel and the anus have become stretched and the boar is unable to take the moist droppings away. Instead, they accumulate into a lump and dry hard, but the boar is still able to bypass the lump with ordinary dry droppings. The lump must always be removed. If this occurs in your cavy, first smear vaseline inside the anus and then after about an hour squeeze the feces out. It will cause some discomfort for a few minutes, but then the boar will be comfortable until it forms a new lump again. A check should be made every few days on the older boars and the feces should be squeezed out to prevent the lump from becoming hard and painful. When the boars have this trouble and are unable to eat droppings, they often begin to deteriorate in health.

Another complaint in adult boars is that the skin or sheath that surrounds the penis can stretch, not allowing the penis to be fully encased within the body. About one-half inch remains outside the body, and where the skin forms into folds, particles of food, hay and sawdust collect in them and cause soreness. A boar in this condition must be examined and cleaned since he will be unable to clean the folds himself. This trouble can cause sterility.

ABORTIONS

Many of the illnesses that bother cavies relate to improper feeding. They are not animals that can adjust to frequent changes in their diets. It is not really known what causes in-pig sows to have abortions, but it is believed that stress and frequent changes in their diets contribute to them.

With some abortions, sows do not lose their entire litters. This is because the carrying of young is divided into two separate sections of the uterus. When one is lost, if the sow can gain strength, she will carry on with the pregnancy and have either one or maybe two young ones at the full term.

When sows have miscarriages or abortions the loss of

blood is excessive and if they do survive, they are very ill. They should be placed in isolation in case it was a contagious abortion and would affect every in-pig sow in the caviary. After such an illness sows need at least two months of rest to gain strength before you consider breeding them again.

A sow can become ill and die a few days after giving birth. This is usually the result of some internal damage caused through the delivery of the young.

With premature births, sows are usually very weak. Occasionally some of the litters will survive, but most that are born are weak, short-haired and very tiny. Premature births are illnesses for sows and are often caused by frights, loud noises and diet changes.

STILLBIRTHS

Stillbirths are one of the greatest losses in the breeding of cavies; they often occur with difficult births. Sometimes it is caused from breeding sows that are either too young or too old to be carrying their first litters. In the young sow prolapsis often occurs; the sow has difficulty in delivering her young, because her body is too small. With continual straining the uterus drops (prolapsis) and as the young are born it protrudes outside the vagina and the sow must be destroyed. Stillbirths in older sows are usualy caused by what is called dystocia. Dystocia means that the sow is unable to deliver her young. This is caused by the young being too large for delivery. This is thought to be caused by excessive protein feeding. The sow's muscles are unable to stretch sufficiently and the pelvic bones are set.

When a sow has had a first litter the necessary stretching remains permanent. Nothing can be done to save the sow if the young are too large to be born. If the sows are operated on for a Caesarian section, they are usually very ill and their chances of survival are not very high. Sows in both the younger and the older age groups that have litters for the

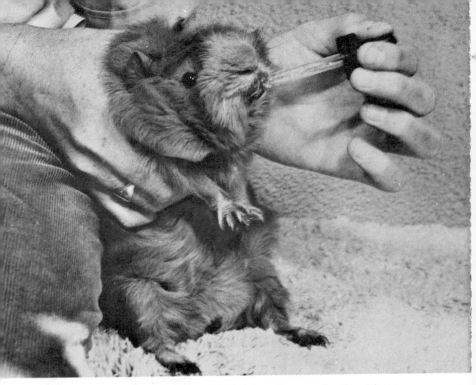

Medicines and supplements are administered conveniently with an eyedropper. Photo by L. van der Meid.

first time also die from the young twisting in the uterus so that the young will not be able to be born head first.

Toxemia causes the death of in-pig sows in the later stages of pregnancy. A sign of this complication is that in-pig sows that were previously active are sitting huddled, refusing food and water. There are only feeble movements of the unborn young ones. There is no known cure for it. It also affects the liver and the sows usually do not live longer than a day or so.

ABSCESSES AND CYSTS

Abscesses and cysts must not become confused with one another. The most common place for an abscess is in the throat and it is called cervical acenitis. It is usually caused by a thistle from hay that has penetrated the inside of the mouth or throat. It becomes infected from contamination by rat or mouse droppings. The abscess takes up to three weeks to develop after the first sign of slight swelling. It swells rapidly and can reach the size of a fist, although the cavy will continue to be active and to eat and drink. It is best to apply hot pads; these must be tested for the right temperature on the back of your hand. When you can see where the abscess will come to a head (the pus will be seen through the skin), make a small cut with the edge of a sterilized razor blade. Apply warm, damp cotton to clear away the pus, which will come out excessively. Watch that your cavy does not shake its head while you are holding it or the pus will be scattered around.

If the abscess breaks while the cavy is in the hutch, the hutch must be cleaned and disinfected because the pus is very foul-smelling. Bathe the open wound in the neck for several days with diluted antiseptic until the skin heals. Abscesses can also occur on the body where skin that was torn during a fight has become infected. These will need the same cleansing attention.

Cysts are very different, being similar to a wen (small, harmless tumor) that affects human beings. They can appear on any part of the body. Some stay the size of a pea while others grow to the size of a walnut. They do not seem to cause distress. Your cavy should not be destroyed because it has cysts.

When sows are handled during judging, cysts will often be seen at the entrance to the bladder. These do, in time, cause distress when a sow urinates; at this stage it will begin to deteriorate in health. Another type of cyst comes up like a small abscess and bursts, then completely clears up. Some fanciers take their cavies to a veterinary surgeon to have the cysts removed. This is a simple operation and does not harm the cavy.

MIDDLE EAR INFECTION

A middle ear infection and a wry neck in a cavy must not

become confused, as both cause the cavy to carry its head to one side. A cavy with infected middle ears tilts its head so that it becomes lop-sided and has difficulty in walking. When a cavy is in this state it is best to destroy it to prevent the infection from spreading. It generally occurs in adult cavies.

WRY NECK

Wry neck is a deformity in new born cavies. It is believed to be hereditary. Do not kill off any that are deformed as soon as they are born. If they are very badly deformed they have to lie on their backs to suckle because they are not able to turn their heads. You will see that those with only a slight deformity of wry neck will appear normal after two days.

MOUTH TROUBLES

A cavy that has had its front teeth broken off during a fall will need a special diet until the teeth have grown sufficiently to allow it to pick up food with them again. This will take about one week.

It will need soft food such as grated beetroot, carrot, sweet apple, bread and milk, crushed oats, mash, short pieces of grass and some hay. Water must be available; if the cavy cannot drink, place the spout of the water drinker in its mouth. Once it is able to get food into its mouth, it will be able to use the back grinding teeth. The cavy will lose considerable condition until the teeth begin to grow and it can eat sufficiently.

There are two forms of mouth disease. One is very contagious and the cavies should be destroyed as the disease quickly spreads. The cavies have sores and scabs around the mouth. In advanced stages these run up into the nose, affect the gums and cause the teeth to become brittle. This form of the disease is incurable. It is caught from infected food dishes, water drinkers and the wire hutch fronts. All must be sterilized if an outbreak occurs.

If a cavy is in poor condition check to see if it is suffering from a mouth disease, as it will be unable to eat sufficiently. Some fanciers apply gentian violet, ointments and oils, but with this disease it is best to destroy the cavy.

The other form of the disease affects the sides of the mouth and is curable. You will see it as a weeping sore or crusty scabs but it will not spread around the mouth. It is caused by food lodging under the flaps of skin at the sides of the mouth. An accumulation of beetroot juice can cause it, when the food sets up an irritation and it develops into a sore. The sides of the mouth must be washed with cotton soaked in warm water. The infected sores must be bathed clean; then iodine can be applied. The sore must be kept dry and any scabs must be removed. It will usually clear up quickly. Never apply any antibiotic around the mouth because it may contain penicillin which would kill your cavy if it were to lick it off.

A good source of Vitamin A is carrots. Cavies love to munch on this crunchy vegetable. Photo by M. F. Roberts.

The teeth should be examined regularly for abnormalities. Jagged edges should be filed to avert feeding troubles later. Photo by M. F. Roberts.

EYE COMPLAINTS

Eye complaints usually occur when the cavy gets hay seeds in its eye. Bathe the eye with a lotion made of one teaspoonful of boric acid powder and one-third pint of warm water. Bathe the eye several times each day. An eye or ophthalmic ointment is widely used by fanciers.

When a young cavy's eye is sore and weeping, it is usually caused by hairs growing from a cyst on the eyelid. The cyst must be removed by a veterinary surgeon or the cavy must be destroyed, as it will be in pain otherwise.

Sometimes when boars are placed together on the judging table (and sometimes sows together) their eyes fill up with a white fluid. This is not a fault or a disease. The judge should wipe it away; it is caused by the scent of a cavy of the same sex.

207

FEET AILMENTS

A very painful complaint called pododermitis occurs on the front feet. At first, the cavy will limp. When you handle your cavy you will then find a bleeding sore that is deeply rooted on the pad of the foot. The sore will be surrounded by very white tissues. The foot will become very swollen and will resemble a mole's foot. The cavy will be unable to walk on it and will spend a great deal of time resting it from the pain. At times this sore forms like an abscess and breaks through the top of the foot and you can see a hole through to the pad.

The foot should be bathed in warm water containing a suitable antiseptic, then covered with gauze and bandaged, like a boot with adhesive tape.

It takes a long time for the foot to heal. It will really need a light covering over the sore until healing has occurred; otherwise pieces of hay, cereals and particles of droppings get attached to the oozing sore. After the foot has healed, where there had been excessive swelling the toes will remain twisted to one side, as if the tendons had been damaged.

HEART ATTACK

Heart attacks can occur in cavies. You can be feeding your cavies in block hutches and one will be waiting on the litter board to be fed. All of a sudden it can tip over to one side and when you pick it up, it gasps and dies. This has happened at cavy shows and often occurs in cavies that are in the best condition.

VITAMIN C DEFICIENCY

Some cavies are seen to be gradually wasting away. This could be from a vitamin C deficiency. This form of the illness is more noticeable in the winter months when there is a shortage of green food that supplies this vitamin.

Cavies must have a daily supply of green food and roots to obtain vitamin C. This vitamin is not stored in the body and they cannot be expected to live very long without it. Ascorbic acid tablets or powder—which is vitamin C—can be added to the drinking water or sprinkled over mash or root feed. It must not be used indefinitely. A fifty-milligram tablet when crushed is sufficient for eight cavies.

RESPIRATORY TROUBLES

The "chirping or singing" cavy is not heard very often in the caviary. When it is, fanciers wonder if the cavy is ill. The noise causes terror and alarm to other cavies who will rush for cover to the corner of their hutches. It is a strange noise coming from the back of the throat and it sounds like a very high-pitched chirp. The sound also terrifies the cavy that is making it; the more alarmed it gets, the higher the pitch goes.

When the noise is being made it appears to have something to do with the back grinding teeth as the movements are from side to side in the jaw, unlike the rattling anger motion of up and down. There has never been a definite reason given as to why the cavy makes this chirping noise. It seldom occurs and then only in a single cavy.

You should spend sufficient time in the caviary, especially in the winter months, to see that all are alert and ready for their food. Listen for unusual noises such as feeble grunts that could be evidence of stomach troubles. Coughing and gurgling in the nose are the first signs of bronchial trouble and in bad cases there would also be a rattling noise along with breathing difficulty. This usually leads to pneumonia. It is best to isolate any cavies that are suffering from colds and bronchial troubles to avoid their spreading.

The cavies should be housed where there is even temperature and if hutches are not available they can be made comfortable in ventilated cardboard boxes. The inner sides should be smeared with eucalyptus oil and the lid closed so that they can inhale the fumes. This will relieve their cold and bronchial miseries.

A cavy is very miserable if its hair is sticky, so do not rub anything on its chest. Generally, there is a slight watery discharge from the nose during a cold and your cavy will rub its nose with its front feet to clear it. Apply one of the mentholated ointments around the nostrils and on the inside of the front legs where there is bare skin that leads from the foot. When applied there, as the cavy tries to wipe the ointment off of its nostrils it will at the same time be re-applying ointment from its foot.

DIARRHEA

When an acute outbreak of diarrhea occurs, take it as a warning, as it can be the start of a contagious disease that could destroy your whole stud.

One of the diseases, salmonellosis, is dreaded by any cavy fancier. It is transmitted by rats and mice that contaminate the food and the hay. Diarrhea may not be one of the first signs of salmonellosis as it strikes in many different ways. Sometimes a few cavies become ill and die, followed by other rapid deaths. By this time, the veterinarian should have been called in. If the disease is confirmed, all ill cavies should be destroyed and burned because there is no cure for them. Should any recover they would only be carriers of the disease.

Mucomycosis is caused by feeding musty and moldy hay. This could also kill off an entire stud. Another disease of this type, called gastroenteritis, has similar symptoms; there is acute diarrhea, dehydration, and death follows. Isolation of any sick animal is very important.

Coccidiosis also causes diarrhea, but not all cavies die. They do lose condition and appetite and will have very little energy. Re-infection can occur from soiled bedding and contaminated food.

In any form of diarrhea, cleanliness is essential.

HEATSTROKE

Heatstroke is usually caused when cavies are confined in

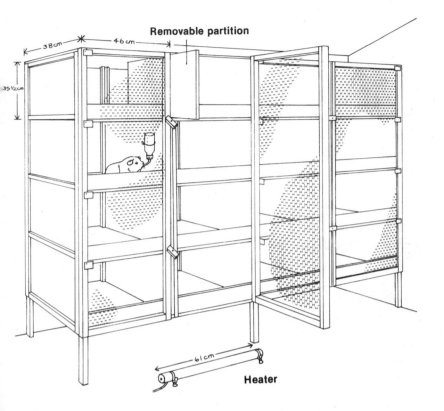

Removable partition

38cm

46cm

35½cm

61cm

Heater

Construction plan of a multi-compartmented hutch for a cavy shed. It is well ventilated and, if needed, the living area can be increased by removing the partitions.

boxes that are too small and have insufficient ventilation during transportation in very hot weather. Often, the cavy will be wet with saliva over the chest and death usually follows. The effect of heatstroke is also seen during the summer on hot days in the caviary. The chests will be wet and this is a warning that they must be moved to cooler surroundings.

Sometimes, cavies will be found paralyzed in the hindquarters and back legs. Fanciers prefer to destroy them because even after recovery they are of little use in breeding.

MITES AND LICE

A skin eruption will cause a cavy to scratch continuously. This is usually evidence of lice or mites. It should be washed with a medicated shampoo. Prescriptions, in powder or spray form, can be obtained from a veterinarian for the control of these parasites. With the exposure of your cavies to other cavies at a show, it is a good idea to spray them when you return from the show.

The mites that burrow under the skin of cavies cause much distress and irritation to them. It is much harder to eradicate mites than it is to get rid of lice. Very many remedies have been used against mites. Some fanciers have found a good remedy while the mites keep re-appearing with others, even after washing their cavies and disinfecting the hutches.

In exhibition cavies the hair is sometimes pulled out in the middle of the back and there will be a small sore; this is known as a broken back or coat. The general belief is that it is caused by lice or mites. Just wash the cavies or their bare patches at weekly intervals until the hair begins to grow back.

Most illnesses stem from poor management on the part of the cavy fancier. Poor sanitation, stale food, moldy and musty hay, and a poor diet all lead to sickness in the caviary. Fanciers have a true obligation to their cavies check for signs that the management of the caviary is not up to par.

Genetics

by Catherine Elizabeth Whiteway

You may wonder why cavies come in such a variety of colors and have long or short coats. Perhaps you have seen that baby cavies are sometimes a different color from that of their parents, and want to know how this can happen. Color and type of coat are almost entirely controlled by inherited factors known as genes, and the study of these factors is called genetics.

The way in which the factors work, and how they are passed from parent to offspring, has been studied in great detail but all we need to know is that each sexually producing organism carries inherited factors in pairs. Parents pass one of each pair of factors to every one of their offspring, who have an equal chance of inheriting either factor. Which factor of a parent's pair is passed on to each offspring is a matter of chance (except in cases of "linkage" which need not concern us here). The factors behave in ways known as dominant, recessive or intermediate.

The factors or genes come to the offspring almost always as exact copies of their parents' genes. But just occasionally an imperfect copy is made, (mutation has taken place) in the processes of cell division needed before reproduction occurs. These inexact copies produce individuals or offspring known as mutants.

AGOUTI PATTERN
Some of the genes control color and coat type, and where they have been recognized they have been given names and

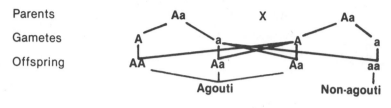

INHERITANCE OF AGOUTI FACTOR

Parents   **Aa**   X   **Aa**

Gametes   **A**   **a**   **A**   **a**

Offspring   **AA**   **Aa**   **Aa**   **aa**

Agouti   **Non-agouti**

symbols. One of the most important of the known genes is the one which causes the Agouti pattern. It behaves as a dominant and the symbol is a capital **A.** Any cavy may have two **A** factors, or one, **A** factor or no **A** factor. As every animal has its factors in pairs, the cavies with one **A** gene, or none, have to have the other partner in the **A** family. This is the recessive gene, symbol **a,** which confers a non-agouti coat to an **aa** animal. **AA** and **Aa** animals, however, are both agoutis, as a result of the dominant effect of **A.** "Dominant" has no reference to the temperament or health of the animal; it refers only to the action of its genes. A recessive gene like **a** can express itself only when present in duplicate. **Aa** animals are said to be "carrying" **a,** but they do not express it.

You may have seen an agouti-patterned cavy. Each hair is banded with two different colors, black and red in the Golden Agouti, black and white in the Silver Agouti, and brown and white in the Cinnamon Agouti. (The last color combination should not really be called that!) Geneticists have usually reserved the name Cinnamon for an Agouti with brown and golden bands. In Agouti cavies even the belly fur is banded but the golden, red, or white band is wider than the black or brown band.

Agouti coloring has some interesting features. It was the color of the wild ancestor of our domestic cavy. The banded hairs are the result of a "switch on, switch off, switch on" process in the pigment-producing cells, which normally functions perfectly all the cavy's life. The pigments, you will notice, fall into two groups. The first group contains black and brown. The ground color, the basic color of the cavy, can be one of the other. The skin and eyes are black when the ground color is black. With brown ground color the skin is pinkish brown and the eyes dark "ruby." Ruby eyes look dark brown, or even blue, in bright light, but in a subdued light they have a red glow. The second group of colors contains red, yellow, cream and even white. The agouti-pattern gene acts by "switching on" first the ground color, then the red-group color, and so on. The red-group colors can be produced in the coat by a different family of genes as well, a family which I will describe later.

NON-AGOUTI PATTERN

The non-agouti partner in this family of genes, symbol **a,** is interesting too. Since agouti is the "wild color" **a** may represent one of the first mutations in the wild and newly-domesticated populations. The same mutation can occur more than once, though completely new mutations have occurred, some of these have given new cavy colors. Non-agouti colors in cavies include Self Black, Self Chocolate, Self Beige and Self Lilac. All of these are **aa,** with other genes at work as well. You may have seen cavies with a patchwork of agouti color and another, perhaps red, golden or cream. The other color is present because of a gene in another series, **E,** and its recessives **e^P** and **e.** The **E** series genes interact with agouti in a remarkable way. At first it looks like another case of dominance but, as two different series are involved, it is not. Cavies with **A** (either **AA** or **Aa**) and **E** show the agouti pattern. **A** with **e^P** gives a mixture of agouti and yellow, red or cream patches. **A** with **ee** gives an all-over red, yellow or cream cavy, while one with **aa** and **ee** is also a uniform red, yellow or cream cavy. The recessive **e** has to be present in duplicate: when it is, it does not matter whether the agouti series genes present are **AA,** **Aa** or **aa** because in each case the cavy looks exactly the same. The **ee** pair of genes prevent all color in the black and brown group from appearing, leaving only the red and yellow group colors in the coat.

You will have noticed that there are three members of the **E** series of genes. This is because two separate mutations of the original **E** gene have occurred. But because the genes are always present in pairs, one inherited from the father and one from the mother, only two of the possible three genes can be represented in each animal. Though its symbol is a capital letter which suggest that **E** is dominant, I have found that it is not completely so, and in practice while **EE** animals are totally non-red, **Ee** ones and **Ee^P** ones may have a little red on the body, face, or feet. Mixed **e^{P}e** cavies have a lot of red or yellow color, more than **e^{P}e^P** ones, but both types vary a lot in individual markings.

The distinction between red-group colors and the non-red is important. All shades from deep red to palest cream are produced by one pigment and all blacks, browns and paler versions of these (like lilac and beige) are produced by a different pigment. Some genes control the degree to which each kind of pigment is produced: sometimes they prevent any from being made at all.

Where intensity of color is reduced by the action of genes, the big **C** group is usually at work. There is some doubt as to how many members of the **C** series there are! Certainly we know **C** itself: it is fully dominant to the recessive in its series and it allows both kinds of pigment to develop fully. So we can have **A C E,** an intense (golden) agouti, and **A** (or **aa**) **C ee,** intense red. Reduced intensity of red-group color is characteristic of **c^d**, which is recessive to **C**. While black and brown are slightly diluted by **c^d**, red is reduced to buff, fawn or cream. The tendency to favor one pigment at the expense of the other is shown by other recessives in this series, too. Next comes **c^r**, which acts like the chinchilla factor in rabbits. Black and brown are very little affected in **c^{r}c^r** cavies, but all red or yellow pigment is inhibited. Now if a cavy has, besides $c^r c^r$, the **E** gene or even e^p, he can develop black or brown all over (with **E**) or in patches. But what if he is **ee**, and what of the red or yellow patches normally found in e^p specimens? Here, black or brown have already been prevented from developing, and now the yellow is inhibited too. There is no pigment left: the fur is pure white. However, the eyes remain dark, usually black or "ruby."

One of the most remarkable of cavy colors is the one like the Siamese cat. Here, another **C** series recessive is at work. In $c^h c^h$ cavies all the red or yellow is absent and the black or brown is both reduced in intensity and restricted to certain parts of the body. The eyes are bright pink. In Black Himalayans the body is white and the ears, nose and feet are very dark drown, nearly black. In Chocolate Himalayans the ears, nose and feet are milk chocolate brown. Because of the name, Himalayan, given to the varieties produced by this gene I prefer to write its symbol c^h, but it is often referred to as c^a. Perhaps this is because in **ee** cavies, where black and brown are already inhibited, the addition of two c^h genes result in a pure white animal with pink eyes, often called an albino. But since the albino coloring in cavies is caused by the interaction of **ee** with the Himalayan genes. These cavies are born pure white, but in a day or two the skin of the nostrils, ears, and foot pads begins to darken, and later the hairs grow darker too. When it is about six months old the cavy's points are as dark as they will ever be.

Another series, **P**, contains a diluting factor as well. At this stage we cannot ignore the small but important **B** series either. In animals with **B**, the dominant, the eyes and skin are black (or diluted black, if a **C** series recessive is present), so that, for instance, while **A B C E** is a Golden Agouti, **A B $c^r c^r$ E** gives a Silver Agouti. The other member of this series is **b**, the recessive, giving a brown or chocolate colored coat, ruby eyes and brown or (in diluted animals) pink skin. To return to the **P** series: the dominant is present in animals with normal fur and eye color, but the recessive **p** in duplicate confers a reddish pink eye color on animals whose eyes would normally be dark. Pink-eyed white animals may have **pp** without any extra effect. Himalayans' pink eyes are due to $c^h c^h$ alone, however. As well as affecting eye color, **pp,** reduces black pigment to a soft grey shade, as found in the Self Lilac, and dilutes chocolate to beige. In contrast to **C** series diluting genes, the **p** gene leaves red and yellow almost unaffected. Reds with **pp** are called Self Goldens in the United Kingdom the color being known elsewhere as Red-Eyed Orange. Pink-Eyed Creams and Agoutis are also known.

We have already seen that an all-white cavy can be produced by c^r or c^h and **e,** and that c^r with e^p gives an animal patched with white, but there is also a single factor which produces white markings on cavies. This is **s.** The dominant, **S,** is present in whole-or self-colored animals, while **Ss** ones often have a little white on the face or feet. Some **Ss** and most **ss** cavies have more white, usually in the form of a blaze on the face, white feet and white bands or patches on the body. One remarkable combination is that of **ss** with $e^p e^p$ and **aaBB,** black. With **C,** this would be the black-red-white tricolor, known as the Tortoiseshell and White, and with the c^d dilution it would give a black-cream-white tricolor. You may be able to work out some of the other combinations.

An unusual effect, which at first looks like the product of **Ss** or **ss,** is given by the new mutant **Rs.** When one of these genes is present (the other being the recessive, **rs**) the animal has its normal color blotched and broken up by white patches. The face and sometimes the feet have white markings, while the body has colored, white and roan areas. Roan is a mixture of white and colored hairs, as seen in horses and cattle. Some animals have solid or roan spots on a white ground and are known as Dalmatians. More heavily

218

marked animals, with plenty of roan and as little white as possible, are called Dapples. **RsRs** animals are white all over, so that the marked **Rsrs** ones are examples of the effect known as intermediate dominance. There is another form of roan, usually darker and more even, and lacking white markings, which is the product of a "silvering" gene. This has been given the symbol **si**, indicating a recessive or semi-recessive behavior, but in my stock I believe that it behaves as a dominant. Occasionally, among these Silver-Roans, a pure white individual turns up. The roaning and silvering factors are still not fully understood, but they produce some attractive cavies.

All these colors can be found in smooth short-haired cavies, or long-haired ones like Peruvians, and in the sort with rosettes all over the body, known as Abyssinians—why, I do not know. Our domestic cavy has its origins in South America. There is also the Crested cavy, with a smooth coat and a single rosette on the forehead. The crest is given by a single dominant gene, Star (symbol **St**), while the multiple rosettes of Abyssinians are due to the interaction of two genes. Long hair is said to be due to a single recessive gene, as in cats, but some fanciers believe that there may be two genes which work together to produce the full-length Peruvian coat.

In the case of Abyssinians and perhaps Peruvians, where two or more genes acting together produce the desired effect, it is possible to have partly-Abyssinian or partly-Peruvian types of animals. These often make very pretty pets. Intermediate forms such as these, and varieties like the Dalmatian, produced by a gene with intermediate dominance, should not mislead cavy breeders into thinking that any pair of cavies will produce offspring midway in appearance between the parents. This result is unusual, and even when it occurs it is due to the action of defined units of hereditary material, the genes. In controlled crossbreeding it can be shown that where a certain number of genes, with known behavior, are present in each parent, the off-spring carry and express the genes in predictable ways—sometimes in new combinations, although making use of only the genetic material passed on by the parents. When two purebred cavies of the same variety are paired up they normally produce offspring of the same color and type as themselves, and if they do not, their own genetic make-up could be less "pure" than was first thought. Pet cavies are often of mixed breeding, with long- and short-haired kinds and many different colors all contributing, to produce a rainbow collection of offspring. Even with such crossbred cavies it is possible to work out which genes must be present, using their own appearance and that of their youngsters as clues in a puzzle. Once you know something about the genetic make-up of your cavies, you can begin to predict what their offspring will be like. Then it is only a short step to planning pairings which will give exactly the colors and types which you would most like to have.

Epilogue

The sorrows, disappointments and pleasures connected with the breeding of cavies have all been discussed—there is no more to add. This has been based on fifty years experience with them.

Many fancier friends have been acquired, including Miss Joan Radeglia, whose name is known in every country that has common interest in cavies. The author has known her for thirty years and is proud to have her as a critic.

Through the many years the mainspring of our hobby has been devotion to the guinea pig or cavy.

ILLUSTRATIONS
INDEX

221